WORKING WITH DISTRESSED PHYSICIANS

A Guide For Physician Leaders

✦

CHARLES R. STONER, DBA
JENNIFER ROBIN, PhD

American Association for
PHYSICIAN
LEADERSHIP

13   8 7 6 5 4 3 2 1

Copyedited, typeset, indexed, and printed in the United States of America

PUBLISHER
Nancy Collins

PRODUCTION MANAGER
Jennifer Weiss

DESIGN & LAYOUT
Carter Publishing Studio

COPYEDITOR
Patricia George

ABOUT THE AUTHORS

Charles (Chuck) R. Stoner, DBA

Chuck Stoner is professor emeritus of management and leadership at Bradley University and president of Stoner & Associates Consulting.

Over the past decade, Chuck's scholarship and consulting have focused on healthcare organizations, with a special emphasis on physician leadership. In this context, his work with physician leaders has included leadership development workshops for a range of healthcare organizations, including Indiana University Health, OSF Healthcare, the University of Illinois College of Medicine, Illinois Cancer Care, and Compass Oncology. Through this work, he has collaborated with more than 500 physician leaders.

Additionally, Chuck has served as faculty facilitator and executive coach in the Business of Medicine Program at Indiana University, a preeminent MBA program designed specifically and exclusively for physicians. In these roles, he has guided hundreds of high-caliber physicians during their leadership journeys.

An early proponent of executive coaching, Chuck has engaged in extended one-on-one coaching relationships with scores of physicians at various stages of their leadership journeys. These physician leaders represent a diverse range of healthcare organizations and practices that include Cedars Sinai, Mayo Clinic Health System, Norton Healthcare, Unity Point Health, AMITA Health, Good Samaritan Hospital, Premier Health, and several others.

Chuck earned his doctorate from Florida State University, majoring in business management and minoring in social psychology. His academic and consulting activities have focused on leadership and organizational behavior, emphasizing the behavioral and interpersonal skills that differentiate thriving leaders from those who struggle. He concentrates on encouraging, enhancing, and empowering leaders to understand and enact difference-making behaviors that are critical for navigating the complexities of contemporary healthcare.

Chuck especially enjoys working with newer and emerging physician leaders who are transitioning from successful clinical careers to expanded roles as leaders, where success comes from working collaboratively with and through others.

An award-winning teacher, researcher, and author, as well as a sought-after speaker, facilitator, and coach, Chuck has been recognized throughout his career for both his teaching and his scholarship, culminating with Bradley University's Presidential Appreciation Award.

He has authored 13 books on business and leadership, as well as numerous refereed academic papers. His most recent books include *Inspired Physician Leadership* (published by the Association for Physician Leadership) and *Building Leaders: Paving the Path for Emerging Leaders*. Both books were co-authored with Jason Stoner.

Chuck and his wife Julie have two sons, Jason and Alex. An avid daily runner, Chuck has logged more than 75,000 miles to date.

Jennifer Robin, PhD

Jennifer Robin, PhD, is a psychologist, ICF credentialed (PCC) Certified Co-Active Coach (CPCC), and an expert in leadership development, organizational culture, and strategic human resource management.

More than 25 years ago, Jennifer was involved in launching one of the first MBA programs designed for physician leaders, working as part of the team that created its leadership development and coaching components at the University of Tennessee. Today, she is an affiliate faculty member and coach with the Business of Medicine program at Indiana University, continuing her impact in healthcare through its leaders.

As a consultant at Great Place to Work® Institute, Jennifer worked with senior leadership teams at several large healthcare organizations in California, Florida, Illinois, and Iowa. She has designed leadership development modules for healthcare organizations, advised major staff units such as human resources and advancement, and worked with system-level leadership to create great workplace cultures. Scripps Healthcare and Mayo Clinic were featured in Jennifer's books: *No Excuses: How You Can Turn Any Workplace into a Great One* (2013) and *The Great Workplace: How to Build It, How to Keep It, and Why It Matters* (2011).

Jennifer works with organizational leaders at all levels and in a broad range of industries. As a consultant, she advises senior leaders as they integrate their organization's culture with its strategy and align efforts to be a great workplace. In her coaching practice, Jennifer guides leaders in career milestones (such as job searches, career changes, transitioning into a new leadership role) and in providing a platform for leadership development in the context of one's current role.

Jennifer earned her PhD in industrial/organizational psychology from the University of Tennessee. Prior to the launch of her coaching and consulting practice, she served as the dean of the School of Business at Southern Connecticut State University and associate dean and professor of management at Bradley University.

TABLE OF CONTENTS

ABOUT THE AUTHORS iii

PROLOGUE xi

PART 1
FOUNDATIONS

CHAPTER 1

Setting the Stage 3

Purpose and Focus 4

The Context for Physician Leadership 6

Previews of Coming Attractions 8

CHAPTER 2

Pinpointing Our Target Physicians 11

Searching for a Meaningful Definition 12

A Legacy of Tolerance 14

The Impact of Unchecked Disruptive and Unacceptable
Physician Behavior 17

Summary Checklist 18

CHAPTER 3

You Are Here 21

Multifaceted Impacts 21

   – Individual Skills and Training 22

   – Individual Circumstances 23

   – Patient Dynamics 23

   – Team Dynamics 24

   – Leader Skill and Experience 24

   – Team Diversity 25

   – Industry Trends 26

Systems Theory 28

Respond; Don't React 31

Summary Checklist 32

CHAPTER 4

Are They Really That Different? 35

Physician Characteristics 36

Physicians and Disruptive Behavior: A Darker Side 38

Facing Reality 41

And of Course ... Context Makes a Difference. 41

Summary Checklist 42

CHAPTER 5

Preparing to Engage with Your Target Physician 43

Physician Leaders as Coaches 43

Building a Coaching Relationship 45

The Coach's Mindset. 46

The Coach's Self-Awareness and Perspective-Taking. 50

Balancing Development and Action 53

Summary Checklist 54

PART 2
CONVERSATIONS AND ACTION STEPS

CHAPTER 6

The Conversation 57

Early Intervention. 57

The Communication Process: The First Message 60

Focus and Limit the Agenda 63

A Blueprint for the Next Step: Coaching. 63

Additional Considerations for a Formal Conversation 65

– Pace 66

– Tone 67

– Understanding 68

Circling Back to Expectations and Needs 69

Summary Checklist 70

CHAPTER 7

Moving to Action **71**

    The Evidence 72

    The Action-Planning Process 75

    A Structured Approach 76

    Consequences and Ramifications 79

    A Winding Path of Growth and Development 81

    The Next Best Step 83

    Summary Checklist 85

CHAPTER 8

Areas for Growth **87**

    A Foundational Perspective 88

    Enhancing Self-Awareness 89

    Impulse Control 91

    Building Empathy. 93

    Apologies 96

    Rebuilding Trust. 97

    Summary Checklist 98

CHAPTER 9

The Rest of the Team **99**

    Winning Teams. 100

    Team Leadership. 108

    Summary Checklist 109

CHAPTER 10

When Is It Finally Enough? **111**

    A Lack of Success Is Not a Failure 112

    The Game Has Changed 113

    And Once Again…The Rest of the Team 116

    Lessons of Leadership 118

    Summary Checklist 119

CHAPTER 11

Conclusions 121

What If the Target Physician Is a Friend? 122

What If the Target Physician Is a Disruptive Boss? 124

How Can I Assert Myself and Have Respectful Disagreements? . . . 126

How Do I Navigate the "Why Me?" Question? 128

How Do I Stem the Tide of Negativity? 129

A Final Perspective 130

Summary Checklist 130

REFERENCES 133

PROLOGUE

FOR THE PAST 15 YEARS, we have been asked to work with physicians who were described as struggling, troubled, distressed, and disruptive. The concerns were never about these physicians' clinical competencies; rather, and not surprisingly, they revolved around interpersonal and interactive behavioral deficiencies that led to tension and stress in the workplace. We were asked to help because the physician's style of working with others had fostered a stressful, uncomfortable, and at times toxic effect on colleagues, staff, and the team-focused culture.

We are behavioral scientists, not physicians. We enter the picture when concerned physician leaders turn to third-party intervention, an approach that is certainly reasonable and understandable given the ever-growing complexity of demands physician leaders face.

We enter the scene as matters have intensified and deteriorated, and we often are part of a remediation plan. The reality is that we are called upon because problems have grown and become unacceptably disruptive. In short, the concerns we will address have been apparent for some time. Another reality is that bringing in third-party experts adds an additional, unfortunately disruptive label and is almost always coupled with increased defensiveness from the distressed physician.

Given these realities, this book rests on a strong philosophical base — a mindset of sorts. We believe that we are all better off when physician leaders address distressed members of their teams at the local level rather than externally, which adds a further layer of complexity to already troubling circumstances. These localized interventions are most effective when carried out by physician leaders themselves, addressed early, and followed with continuity and ongoing communication.

Yet, we are not naïve to the challenges of a localized intervention. Physician leaders typically struggle with these interactions for two reasons: time and a legitimate concern about what to do, especially as they may lack the skills and approaches to have meaningful, helpful conversations.

As such, the main purpose of this book is to help physician leaders address and work more effectively with physicians who exhibit distressed and disruptive behaviors. We carefully walk through how to approach these conversations, develop a plan of action, enhance skills, and become a partner in developmental support. This can be a daunting task, and our goal is to make it clearer and a bit less ominous.

In addition to reviewing the best research and writing in the field, this book draws from our experiences as well as those of some amazing physicians who have kindly shared with us. Here, we extend a special shout-out of appreciation to Drs. Steve Hippler and Sarah Zallek, who, along with several other physicians, shared experiences and insights that helped us develop and frame this project.

All examples used in this work are real. Most are drawn from our work consulting with physician leaders, as well as coaching target physicians exhibiting unacceptable and disruptive behaviors. In all cases, names have been changed. Additionally, in some cases, areas of specialty may be changed to ensure anonymity. In a few cases, examples are composites, again undertaken to ensure that individuals could not be identified.

A special thanks to Nancy Collins, our editor at AAPL, an amazing sounding board and unparalleled advisor. Nancy's support and guidance have been most appreciated.

For Chuck, my thanks to Jennifer for working with me on our second book project. As always, I appreciate Jen's talents and spirit and the expansive impact as we bounce ideas back and forth. Finally, a heartfelt thank you to Dr. Julia Stoner. As with all adventures over the last 50 years, she has been my foundation of encouragement, support, and unconditional love.

And as for me (Jennifer), I am grateful to Chuck for inviting me to be a part of his next book. Chuck is everything you'd want in a coauthor: creative, lighthearted, and brilliant, all while being an engine to move the project forward. And, a huge thank you to my love, Pablo Navarro, a true renaissance man — sommelier and chef, thought partner, and best friend.

PART 1

Foundations

CHAPTER 1

Setting the Stage

....

DAVE WAS STILL IN HIS SCRUBS, only a few minutes tardy, as we met at a local coffee shop. An hour earlier, he was engaged in his clinical role: the emergency surgical repair of the mangled left arm of an accident victim. Dave was distant, and we could quickly surmise that our scheduled initial coaching session rested near the bottom of his priorities for the day.

"A talented young surgeon" was the consistent statement used by senior surgeons and leaders to describe Dave. One physician colleague noted, "Dave has amazing potential — if he can just stop shooting himself in the foot."

A demanding perfectionist with a sarcastic tone and caustic streak, Dave defended his actions without hesitancy. "I do what I must do to ensure patient safety and successful outcomes. Sure, I have high standards. Who'd want anything less?"

Despite the somewhat combative tone, we refused to take the proverbial bait. Besides, none of the complaints that we'd reviewed questioned his clinical skills. Rather, the complaints stemmed from his harsh and dismissive tone toward nurses and staff. Some but not all of these episodes occurred in the OR.

Poised to begin working with Dave, we understood the fragility of the task. Dave was talented and proud. He basked in his hard-edged professional expertise — a reputation that was frequently buoyed by thankful patients. However, Dave was short on patience, a condition exacerbated by his quick temper, colorful language, perpetual scowl, and commanding physical presence. In a previous era, his behavior may have been tolerated, but that era has passed, and greater sensitivity, even in the high-pressured surgical world, is now expected and demanded.

Adding to the complexity of our coaching interactions, Dave was meeting with us as part of a mandated remediation plan. From his perspective, we were the lesser evil of other options presented to him. In short, Dave's readiness for coaching and change was far from optimal.

How did we get here? How did a young surgeon with such promise and potential end up meeting with external behavioral scientists? Dave had been with the practice for nearly two years, and concerns about him surfaced within the first few weeks. Had any earlier remediation efforts been put in place? Had corrective conversations taken place? Or, had we simply reached a tipping point, a final straw-that-broke-the-camel's-back grievance added to those that had accumulated over the past two dozen months?

What led Dave's physician leader to reach out for help, admitting, "I'm at my wit's end with this guy." How could this have been addressed sooner? And, perhaps most damning, had Dave burned so many bridges and been tagged with so many negative labels that salvaging his career within the practice was problematic at best?

On the surface, Devon was quite different than Dave. While Dave wore a perpetual scowl, Devon smiled easily, consistent with her love for her clinical work, her regard for her patients, and her get-it-done attitude. She took on extra assignments and pushed herself to do more. Like Dave, she was a perfectionist who needed to control the situations she encountered.

Coincidentally, Devon was in the throes of a complicated life away from the hospital. Dealing with health challenges affecting her elderly parents and struggling to connect with an increasingly rebellious teenage son, Devon's emotional reservoir was running low. Three times in the last two weeks, she had sarcastically lashed out at staff members for seemingly minor omissions – omissions that slowed Devon's pace and added another element of stress to her day.

Although each formal complaint was followed by a heartfelt apology, Devon seemed incapable of thwarting her demeaning behaviors when she experienced clinical frustrations or delays. Soon, her apologies failed to attain much of an effect. Her physician leader, an overworked clinician struggling to respond, candidly expressed his concerns, "I'm afraid that when I intervene, I'll push her over the edge." We all recognized that her edge was perilously shaky.

PURPOSE AND FOCUS

While this book is certainly about physicians like Dave and Devon, it is written to provide a helpful resource for physician *leaders* addressing a specific people issue — disruptive behavior — which can be bewildering, intimidating, and seemingly intractable. Our focus is two-fold.

First, physician leaders must recognize, understand, and address physician colleagues whose behaviors have become chronically disruptive. Here, we will create a deeper awareness of the multidimensional nature of workplace behavior, and we will use that awareness to model approaches for early actions to be taken before unfortunate, destructive, and hard-to-change labels become widespread and ingrained. Of necessity, we will also discuss how to constructively intervene with those who are well along the jagged path of disruption.

Of course, helpful intervention is easier said than done. As we work with physician leaders, we are frequently asked pointed interactive questions:

- How do I go about having a meaningful conversation with a physician exhibiting disruptive behavior?
- What do I do when they refuse to accept their behavior and their role in diminishing the work environment?
- What do I do when they disagree, become belligerent, and are aggressively challenging?
- How do I keep them on-task, advancing toward meaningful remediation?
- What is the balance between sensitivity and support and taking a tough, direct, and unequivocal approach?
- When should we escalate our attempts to enact change and include internal committees and human resources?

And there is an additional critical factor that resides just beneath the surface: How do we lead the rest of the staff as we try to address and remediate a single disruptive team member? In the following pages, we will address these concerns to provide you, as physician leaders, with practical, research-based ideas for action.

Second, as noted above, we will present evidence-based ideas on how to establish a working environment where the emergence of disruptive behaviors is modulated or prevented in the future. In this context, we draw from key research and respected thought leaders.

We understand that your healthcare system may restrict, at least to some extent, your capacity for broad, interactive changes. However, as a talented physician leader, there is much that you can do. Here, we will offer guidance. We agree with the perspective offered by the American College of Surgeons that the best approach to dealing with disruptive behavior is to help prevent its development in the first place.[1,2] And we concur with leadership researchers Robert Kegan and Lisa Lahey as they assert, "Leaders who ask themselves, 'What can I do to make my setting the most fertile ground in the world for the growth of talent?' will put themselves in the best position to succeed."[3]

Ultimately, we strive to help physician leaders foster a positive, best-place-to-work culture.[4] As such, teamwork is enhanced, colleague morale is improved, and the emerging culture shifts from toxicity to collective positivity and support.

THE CONTEXT FOR PHYSICIAN LEADERSHIP

In today's healthcare environment, there is no doubt that all physicians are facing unparalleled levels of stress.[5,6] It is the collective context within which physicians practice. Patient demands intensify, and time allotted for direct patient interaction is limited and often externally controlled. Addressing important tasks such as patient notes and charting are pressing and time-consuming responsibilities.

Organizational restructuring, often undertaken in the name of efficiency, leads many physicians to conclude that their work is being overwhelmed by bureaucracy, reducing their sense of control and further removing them from their reasons for entering the profession in the first place.[7]

Exacerbating these concerns are unprecedented staffing shortages among physicians and nurses — concerns that appear likely to intensify in coming years.[8,9] Physician and staff burnout are central concerns, reaching near-crisis levels.[7,10,11] And all of this plays out within what appears to be an overly complicated and uncooperative electronic health record system.[12]

Even this partial list underscores the message that physicians are confronting a confluence of intense and unrelenting stressors. While the stressors noted above are externally imposed, physicians, as a group, place enormous internal demands and expectations on themselves. As such, physician distress is an escalating concern, and mounting evidence indicates that physicians are experiencing unprecedented levels of stress, which too frequently culminate in exhaustion and burnout.[6,13]

In the center of this mix is the physician leader who confronts the interweaving dynamics of a complicated scenario — the proverbial person in-the-middle who is the lynchpin between day-to-day clinical tasks and broader administrative strategy. As such, it's not hyperbole to suggest that the physician leader's role is one of the most demanding within the healthcare setting.

Consider a few examples that illustrate how this maze of challenges plays out. In most cases, physician leaders perform multiple or mixed roles, spending part of their time engaged in their clinical activities and a portion of their time in their role of administrative leadership.[14]

Of course, progressive leaders want to be more than administrative care-takers; they want to create and move their units toward viable, future-focused visions. They strive to integrate their unit's activities with other areas of the healthcare system. They attend to and ensure responsibility for reaching key metrics that are firmly monitored by administrators who may or may not have a clinical background. Perhaps most challenging, the physician leader must encourage and support a team of highly talented, achievement-oriented clinicians who value independence, eschew external controls, and exhibit demanding perfectionist tendencies.

Finally, the leader must help this group of independent thinkers work together and with clinical staff to function as an effective and high-perform-ing team. No wonder leadership guru Warren Bennis noted that leading in such settings is a bit akin to herding cats.[15]

There is no way around it: leadership is difficult and, at times, frustrating. A few years ago, we conducted a series of in-depth interviews with top execu-tives, addressing their experiences of adversity and their actions of resiliency that enabled personal healing and progress. During these exchanges, we asked participants to share their most vexing organizational challenges. In the spirit of rigorous qualitative inquiry, we posed open-ended questions and tried our best to purge any preconceived notions using a robust research model where data drives analysis.[16]

Understandably, there was no unanimity, but it was not far off. These seasoned leaders offered varied examples, colorful stories, and pointed impressions. Yet, one theme prevailed across all respondents: the most try-ing issues were always people issues.

One leader, laden with emotion regarding an event in the distant past, spoke of terminating one of his senior vice-presidents — a man who had been a life-long friend. Another leader expressed his sense of personal disappoint-ment and feelings of ineptitude that he was unable to unravel a damaging conflict between two talented project leaders. Some leaders spoke of feelings of loss and intense disappointment when trusted colleagues engaged in inten-tional disruptive and even unethical behavior. Often, the leaders' examples centered on the same person, time after time. Nearly everyone noted nights of disrupted sleep spent pondering these tricky interpersonal issues.

While leaders experiencing adversity emerged stronger, it was not with-out shouldering a fair amount of stress and drain of personal resources in the process, sometimes shaking the very core of their identity as effective leaders. Later in this book, we discuss research addressing the balance of interpersonal relationships and organizational priorities, known in academic terms as transcollegial leadership.[17]

PREVIEWS OF COMING ATTRACTIONS

In the following chapters, we provide clear, practical, and useable ideas and actions for working effectively and productively with physicians who engage in chronic disruptive behaviors. The first five chapters, which comprise Part 1, work together to provide a solid foundation for addressing the behavioral issues at hand.

More specifically, in Chapter 2, "Pinpointing Our Target Physicians," we will define the individuals of concern — those who display ongoing and unacceptable disruptive behaviors. Further, we will discuss why the oft-practiced approach of tolerance (conflict avoidance) toward these physicians is a problematic path.

In Chapter 3, "You Are Here," we offer a map of the behavioral terrain. Here, we encourage physician leaders to recognize and consider the multiple factors that may affect and lead to disruptive behaviors. Leaders are encouraged to address issues systematically while taking into account the idiosyncratic nature of the challenges ahead.

Chapter 4, "Are They Really That Different?", provides a deep look into the characteristics of our target physicians and contrasts them with the rest of the physician staff. These perspectives offer physician leaders a fundamental understanding and zero-in on target physician preferences that may affect the leader's corrective actions.

In Chapter 5, "Preparing to Engage with Your Target Physician," we talk directly with physician leaders to enhance their engagement and coaching with target physicians. Here, we discuss how physician leaders can use coaching skills to embrace a supportive and developmental mindset.

Part 2 of the book digs into the dynamics of working with distressed physicians through focused conversations and practical action steps. We begin with Chapter 6, "The Conversation." Here, as the title denotes, we detail the essential nature of the developmental conversation. Starting with the power of early intervention, we emphasize how to deliver a needed and effective message.

Chapter 7, "Moving to Action," is a pivotal chapter. Here, we provide tools for the positive engagement, coaching, and developmental support necessary for leaders to achieve appropriate behavioral change among target physicians. The significance and nature of the plan of action are discussed in detail.

In Chapter 8, "Areas for Growth," we emphasize the likely content of developmental conversations and goals. Our focus revolves around issues of emotional intelligence and includes the key themes of delivering apologies and rebuilding trust between the target physician and the rest of the team.

Chapter 9, "The Rest of the Team," offers key insight into helping the rest of the team adjust to work with the target physician and progress as a unified team. This perspective becomes important as the leader works to repair fractured relationships and enhance the desired clinical and behavioral culture.

In Chapter 10, "When Is It Finally Enough?", we confront the reality that despite the leader's best efforts, every target physician cannot be brought into the fold. In practical, bottom-line terms, we address these final decisions with a special focus on the physician leader and the clinical team that remains.

Finally, Chapter 11, "Conclusions," highlights the common questions that we have been asked during our workshop and consulting activities with physician leaders as they address their target physicians. Readers will appreciate the practical and impactful nature of these inquiries.

This is a lofty adventure and one that can be a differentiator for progressive physician leaders. Let's get started!

CHAPTER 2

Pinpointing Our Target Physicians

....

W E HAD WORKED WITH SANDY FOR NEARLY A YEAR. She was a caring physician, and although she held no formal position of authority, her concern for the practice and its future led most colleagues to recognize and accept her role as an informal, difference-making leader. As always, she cut to the chase.

"I'm worried about Nicole, one of our physicians," Sandy shared. "She works at one of our satellite centers, and there seem to be problems." Nicole had been hired eight months earlier after an extensive search, and she filled a key clinical need for the practice.

Sandy continued, "She is behind on her notes. That affects our billing. But even more concerning, she's butting heads with the staff — alienating some of our most senior nurses and laboratory technicians." A pause, and then, "I think I need to do something before this all goes off the rails."

There was another expectant pause as the impact of the matter became evident. Nicole was emerging as a distressed and struggling physician, often displaying disruptive behaviors.

As behavioralists, we cringe at the term "disruptive physician," and with good cause. Consider another scenario: Carl, an experienced anesthesiologist.

Fresh from an internal disciplinary meeting, Carl took the lead in our initial meeting. "First of all, I am not a disruptive physician, and I refuse to accept that designation. I am a very good doctor who follows every best-practice guideline," he said. "I know this can be viewed by some as an impediment, but I will not bend my standards of patient care." Of course, Carl was right.

However, Carl began to recognize through our work together that his adamant and strident approach to upholding those standards often came with a pungent, dismissive, and diminishing tone toward others. In the emotionally charged setting of the OR, Carl fought for respect by demeaning others, often with biting sarcasm.

From a purely clinical perspective, Carl was a good doctor. He was also a doctor who engaged in disruptive behaviors that became increasingly prevalent as the stress of the immediate clinical situation escalated. The important

11

lesson here is that Carl was a talented physician, but he was also a distressed physician who frequently engaged in disruptive behaviors.

This is not an uncommon dynamic: a solid clinician who also engages in unacceptable disruptive behaviors. However, the dichotomy and its consequences challenge and complicate the physician leader's job. In this chapter, we will explore the nature and impact of disruptive behaviors and the physicians who display toxic behaviors that, over time, become chronic.

Throughout the book, we refer to the physicians of concern as *target physicians*. We do so to focus on the person rather than a disruptive label. While our label may be more constructive, we arrived here after untangling multiple, sometimes conflicting, definitions of the behavior demonstrated by our target physicians.

SEARCHING FOR A MEANINGFUL DEFINITION

Let's examine the generally accepted nature of the issues at hand, starting with perspectives provided by the American Medical Association (AMA). The AMA Code of Medical Ethics defines *disruptive behavior* as "any abusive conduct, including sexual or other forms of harassment, or other forms of verbal or nonverbal conduct that harms or intimidates others to the extent that quality of care or patient safety could be compromised."[18]

An important factor within this definition of disruptive behaviors is that they typically occur in situations where physicians hold a power differential over others — nurses, staff, and often even non-physician administrators.[19] In most healthcare organizations, whether in formal leadership positions or not, physicians have implicit power due to their expertise and credentials.[20]

Both the American Medical Association (in the Code of Medical Ethics) and the American College of Surgeons provide an interesting interpretation and key distinction regarding disruptive behavior. These sources agree that physician comments that come from good-faith intentions of improving patient care are generally not included within the realm of disruptive behavior. In short, advocating for patients — even when done with passion and intensity — is not disruptive behavior.[1,2] Of course, such a distinction can be subtle, a matter open to varied interpretations, and, at times, the first step on a precarious slippery slope.

Several sources have attempted to categorize the kinds of behaviors we will be discussing and addressing. For example, Gail Van Norman differentiates *abusive behaviors* (including verbal insults, intimidation, and diminution of others) from *disruptive behaviors* where patients are affected, presenting all of these concerns under the umbrella term of MAD behavior (mean, abusive, and disruptive).[21] This distinction can be helpful. As many physician leaders have experienced, even when patients are not directly affected in a negative manner, abusive actions toward colleagues can undermine the integrity and spirit of the team.

Let's consider another helpful distinction. Stanton Samenow and colleagues distinguish between *aggressive disruptions* (angry outbursts and verbal threats), *passive aggressive, disruptive behaviors* (making derogatory comments), and *passive behaviors* (such as being chronically late for meetings and appointments, producing inadequate chart notes, and refusing to respond to call).[22] Overall, research indicates that the most prevalent actions taken by distressed physicians are those of aggression: verbal threats, angry outbursts, and swearing.[23] Critically, disruptive behaviors often build over time until they become a style of interpersonal interaction, a style that intensifies when not addressed.[24]

For some physicians, the presence of disruptive behaviors may become a chronic pattern. Occasional outbursts, especially when coupled with high-stress situations, may be unfortunate, but they are also understandable. These emotional releases — likely signs of specific instances of emotional exhaustion — are not our direct focus.[25] Rather, a chronic pattern of disruptive activities is the dividing line between disruptive behavior and expressions of frustration within a given set of circumstances.

Let's bring these observations into focus with an example. During early morning hospital rounds, Carlos was pleased to find that his patient was responding positively to the prescribed treatment regimen. Striving for continued progress, Carlos inquired how the patient's aided walks were going. The patient replied that he had not been taken for any walks yet. Carlos pushed further, "Are you telling me that you have not been out of bed? No walks, even brief walks?" Again, the patient responded that no walks had yet occurred.

Concerned for his patient and feeling an inner surge of frustration, Carlos immediately sought out the nurse on duty and forcefully demanded that she "do her job." His tone could easily be described as an angry outburst.

The scenario can be instructive and open to interpretation, and we likely need more information before we entertain questions of intervention and, ultimately, behavior change. Should Carlos have tempered his interactions with the nurse? Should he have practiced the skills of interpersonal communication that allow one to be direct and unequivocal without being rude and dismissive? Perhaps, although we recognize that Carlos' passion and emotion were born of genuine concern for patient well-being. Importantly, was this a somewhat unique event — perhaps one that was followed by an explanatory apology a bit later?

Our concerns intensify when the exhibited behaviors are commonplace, when they become part of Carlos' interactive pattern with nurses and staff, even when prompted by reasonable expectations and resultant frustrations. The key distinction is whether we are dealing with a one-off or occasional behavior versus a chronic pattern.

There is an additional set of considerations. As noted in Chapter 1, all physicians work in the pressure-laden environment of contemporary healthcare. Physicians, like everyone else, occasionally behave in ways that are problematic and unfortunate. This is a dimension of life. We need to look further to define the types of disruptive behavior that help us identify our target physician.

Truly disruptive, problematic behaviors are experienced on one of two levels.[14] First is the *performance outcomes* level, where key outcomes or metrics are negatively affected. Second is the *interpersonal outcomes* level, where the manner or style of interactions blunts the spirit, morale, cohesiveness, and collaborative nature of individuals or the overall team (or both). In other words, negative interpersonal outcomes arise when physicians simply do not seem to be able to work and play well with others.

Given these considerations, we take a somewhat expansive view of disruptive behaviors and target physicians who exhibit such actions. As such, disruptive behaviors are characterized by (1) chronic disruptive (destructive) or unprofessional behavior that (2) negatively affects patient outcomes, key performance metrics, team morale, or the desired collegial culture.

As we will see shortly, these issues are often exacerbated by limited or skewed self-awareness from the target physician, as well as the target physician's inability to self-correct — often due to a lack of impulse control; under-developed communication, conflict, and remediation-oriented skills; and/or the physician's unwillingness to address disruptive behaviors. These issues are often extended by a prevailing administrative system that does not fully and adequately support remedial efforts.

A LEGACY OF TOLERANCE

Physicians who exhibit disruptive behaviors (our target physicians) have always been part of the healthcare landscape. Once viewed as personality quirks arising when high-caliber clinical expertise was coupled with a dominant drive to ensure favorable patient outcomes, these physicians were tolerated — at times grudgingly so.

In part, the logic of tolerance was drawn from an awareness that these physicians frequently possessed clinical skills that enhanced the patient experience and generated important revenue streams. The Tennessee Medical Foundation noted that, in general, physicians exhibiting ongoing disruptive behaviors view themselves as clinically superior to others (a claim that may often be true), see other members of the healthcare team as less competent, and envision themselves as champions for patients and patient care — claims with which patients frequently concur.[24]

Despite these perceptions and whatever legitimacy they may earn, tolerance for disruptive behavior has frayed against our contemporary healthcare backdrop, where respect, support, collegiality, compassion, and teamwork are central values. There are significant concerns about the emotional and litigious effects of failing to address what is perceived by many as a hostile work environment. In addition, the drive for equity, tolerance, and a positive and engaging workplace culture have further shaken the assumptions undergirding the de facto model of tolerance.

Understanding the intellectual limitations of an attitude of tolerance and translating such awareness into remedial behaviors are dramatically disparate undertakings. The research evidence is clear: the prevailing approach most leaders take when confronted with the need for difficult interpersonal conflicts and problematic behaviors is avoidance — doing nothing while hoping against hope that perpetrators will eventually engage in enlightened self-corrective behaviors.[25] At times, such lofty hopes reach fruition. Most often, however, they do not. Accordingly, there is a marked tendency among leaders to avoid addressing disruptive actions until they reach crisis levels.[26]

Choosing to avoid confronting a distressed physician often rests on a logical hope to avoid conflict. As all know so well, conflict, as a stress-inducing event, generates a series of physiological and psychological dynamics — the classic fight-or-flight syndrome.[27]

Commonly, physician leaders are anxious. Their thought and energy patterns are disrupted. And perhaps more importantly, post-encounter stress is likely to prevail as the other party challenges and pushes back. If you have avoided such conflicts, you come by that avoidance honestly due to the stressful nature of interpersonal friction alone.

But, the reasons for avoidance are often even more complicated and nuanced. For example, physician leaders may fear that they lack the necessary interpersonal and behavioral skills to address problematic behaviors, often driven by a fear of making matters worse and potentially driving a talented colleague to leave the practice. These concerns are exacerbated by a general awareness that leaders often lack positive relations with the offenders, thus void of the social capital and earned support needed to address physicians and their disruptive actions.

Regardless of the leader's instinct to avoid addressing the situation head-on, the notion that the target physician will self-correct is a myth. Fundamentally, target physicians typically lack a keen sense of self-awareness and accurate impressions of the true impact their behavior is having on others — themes we will discuss more fully later in this book.[28] And this responsibility to bring awareness to the physician's tendencies, behavior, and reputation compounds the instinct to avoid the conversation altogether.

This becomes the backdrop for a strategy of tolerance, where leaders grouse, shake their heads in disappointment, resign themselves to struggle while hoping for the best, and proverbially "kick the can down the road." This simple response produces complex outcomes. The failure to address problematic behaviors not only stokes discontent but also reinforces (through inaction) actions that fall beyond the scope of acceptability. Further, looking more broadly, "disruptive behaviors are often reinforced within the clinical micro system."[29]

A final factor must be considered. When a physician's disruptive behavior persists, the target physician is likely to experience negative labels from colleagues and staff — labels that can be powerful and destructive. Over time, the label becomes a broadly accepted descriptor, one that can become even more powerful than the positive clinical skills that the physician possesses. Once established, the label as one who deviates from expected norms begins to dominate how others identify with the target physician.[30]

In practice, the label becomes a restrictive lens through which all behaviors are viewed. Consequently, even relatively minor actions by the target physician are colored by the label adopted by others, perceptually, to foster consistency around the label. Labeling theory even suggests that the target physician begins to think and act in accordance with the designated label — a form of self-fulfilling prophecy.[31]

The most powerful way to avoid the negative stereotyping that comes with negative labels is for physician leaders to take remedial action before the label becomes accepted and internalized within the unit. Recall our opening example of Dave. After two years, the negative label assigned to Dave has become damning, has been reinforced, and will be quite difficult to alter or change.

THE IMPACT OF UNCHECKED DISRUPTIVE AND UNACCEPTABLE PHYSICIAN BEHAVIOR

Considerable research provides evidence of the impact of unchecked disruptive behavior. No list is exhaustive, and you can surely add dysfunctional outcomes from your experiences. In this section, we will rely on both research and theoretical perspectives.

First and perhaps most critical, there is a relationship between disruptive physician behavior and undesirable clinical outcomes.[32] Among these concerns, Phillip Hemphill and Marty Martin emphasize that disruptive clinician behavior negatively affects a range of issues, including communication, coordination of care, patient safety, and overall quality of care.[33] Among the perils, as communication wanes in the face of disruptive behavior, the risk of dangerous delays and clinical errors grows.

Our second consideration is drawn from the theory and research of equity theory — a classic interpersonal and motivational perspective — that emphasizes the ongoing evaluative comparisons that we all make.

Professionals are sensitive to concerns of equity and fairness and experience frustration and diminished motivation and performance when they perceive that a logical sense of equity has been violated and allowed to continue.[34,35] As such, when disruptive behavior is unchecked, elements of fundamental equity are threatened. Professional staff conclude, and rightfully so, that the target physician is getting away with behavior that would not be tolerated among those with lesser status and power.

Feelings of inequity and subsequent ongoing tension affect overall staff morale and well-being.[32] Grievances intensify. One CMO shared with us his impression that staff members typically file grievances only when they realize that nothing is being done to address egregious concerns.

Not surprisingly, ongoing disruptive behavior contributes to staff burnout and overall staff health.[36,37] Further, when disruptive behavior persists, staff experience dissatisfaction and increased intention or desire to leave, which can culminate in actual turnover.[38,39] Of course, those who choose to leave are generally quite talented and have the capacity to leave for other opportunities.

A third and often-overlooked consideration is how inaction undermines the fabric of a unit's or practice's culture.[22] Instead of a positive and supportive dynamic, the emerging culture becomes one where trust and collegiality are undermined — far from what progressive organizations desire.[4]

Fourth, in today's litigious environment, legal ramifications must be recognized as possible outcomes of tolerance and inaction toward disruptive behaviors. Among other factors, failure to address disruptive issues increases the likelihood of malpractice and discrimination litigation.[24]

Our fifth point concerns you, the physician leader. Like it or not, you and your leadership effectiveness are being evaluated constantly by others. What you say (and do not say) and what you do (and do not do) are being observed, and impressions are being formed. When you do not address pernicious issues, your credibility and, ultimately, your impact as a leader are diminished. We will address these concerns more fully in our later chapters.

SUMMARY CHECKLIST

We recognize that our readers are busy physicians who are also addressing the challenges of leadership. Time is a critical resource. In response, we will end each chapter with a summary checklist of key themes presented within the chapter. Summary themes for Chapter 2 are:

- Our target physicians are physicians first, but they are also physicians who display chronic unacceptable and disruptive behaviors.
- Unacceptable (disruptive) behaviors are conceptualized as chronic disruptive or unprofessional behaviors that negatively affect patient outcomes, key performance metrics, individual and team morale, or the desired culture of collegiality.
- For a number of reasons, taking a strategy of tolerance toward target physicians is typically problematic.
- Failing to address issues with target physicians may lead to undesirable clinical outcomes, a breach in team members' sense of equity and fairness, plummeting morale, escalating grievances, increasing intentions to turnover, possible legal ramifications, threats to the desired culture of trust and collegiality, and ultimately, diminished perceptions of the physician leaders' credibility.
- Given the above points, we encourage you to accept responsibility for addressing disruptive behaviors. It is part of physician leadership. The sooner you do so, the quicker you can get to work defining your

solution set rather than expending the same amount of energy hoping the situation goes away.

- Choose terms wisely and be careful when labeling people. Focus on the disruptive behaviors, but don't demonize your target physician.

CHAPTER 3

You Are Here

....

AS PHYSICIAN LEADERS, YOU ARE HERE, faced with a physician whose behavior is your responsibility to address. Leaders have some guidelines from the credentialing committee and the hospital's progressive discipline policy; however, what most physician leaders need is a map and an understanding of where they are on that map. This chapter is meant to provide a systems-level view of the target physician's behavior and the leader's points of leverage — where one can exercise control and influence to mitigate circumstances and the tools needed to do so. Let's consider an example.

MULTIFACETED IMPACTS

Jody is a mid-career orthopedic surgeon who has never expressed interest in leadership, even in hospital committee assignments. As a result, she was never given a reason to think deliberately about building trust or influencing others and has underdeveloped conflict management skills. Until now, one of the reasons she was grateful for her job was that she could be relatively certain of her calendar several weeks in advance.

Now, supporting an adult child who is in the middle of a confrontational divorce, Jody has little mental and emotional capacity to handle even the slightest deviation from her schedule. While she will never admit it (even if she is aware of it), that is one reason she has been obstructive and adversarial in adopting temporary call schedule practices.

With two of the six partners moving on, call has been doubled for the foreseeable future, and Jody is not confident a new hire will agree to the previous practice of distributing call responsibilities based on tenure. New hires have a lot more power than they did in her day. The thought of taking on more call temporarily and an increased schedule going forward is disheartening. Setting broken bones in the middle of the night while being expected to calm anxious (and simultaneously angry, depending upon the cause of the broken bone) patients and their loved ones is exhausting at a soul-level.

Compounding the problem, a new director of the Department of Surgery was recently put in place, and he has close relationships with the other three orthopedic surgeons who remain in her practice. Even though she prides herself on being "one of the guys," Jody has always secretly felt like an outsider, a woman in a male-dominated field who does solid work without much need for recognition or fanfare.

Now that she has raised concerns (inelegantly, admittedly), she is getting more of a cold shoulder than usual. One of her peers pointedly suggested in a meeting that anyone not stepping up during a crisis like this was irresponsible. Needless to say, if Jody felt like an outsider previously, she now feels like an outcast.

Jody has neither the time nor the energy to schedule a meeting with the director, but she knows a sit-down with Amit is coming. She is prepared to make the case that more call would guarantee reduced quality and safety for patients. Meanwhile, Amit has been working with his coach on how to approach Jody, and at the end of his last meeting, he was left with a question that is still on his mind: "Where do I intervene? Even though Jody's resistance is a problem, it isn't happening in a vacuum. How can I address the immediate issue while making sure I untangle the causes?"

Amit is on to something. Acknowledging and understanding the multidetermined nature of disruptive behavior is foundational to addressing it. Such thinking is ingrained in physician behavior: assess and then act. In this chapter, we provide leaders with a framework that allows them to see the whole board more clearly rather than focus on one person and their detrimental behavior.

As the short example above illustrates, any individual response (disruptive or not) to an objectionable situation may be determined in part by one or some combination of seven considerations. Let's look at each briefly.

Individual Skills and Training

In the example above, we know that Jody is a mid-career physician (and, therefore, may not have had solid interpersonal skills training in medical school). Further, she has not participated in leadership roles. It is reasonable to assume she has not engaged in any leadership development opportunities. As such, she is likely a highly skilled physician with underdeveloped interpersonal skills. In an increasingly team-oriented approach to units — be they care teams, practices, or academic departments — Jody's experiences (or lack thereof) have not set her up for success.

We know that the scenario that Jody faces is changing. While medical school education has not traditionally focused on the accomplishments of the team, medical schools, and boards are recognizing its impact on quality of care, patient safety, and the well-being of individuals who function as part of care teams.[40,41,42] But, until the medical students of tomorrow enter practices and leadership roles, we may see the instinct to move ahead alone beat out the instinct to move collaboratively as a team.

Individual Circumstances

Jody's life outside of work has not been restorative. In fact, her non-work demands and responsibilities have further diminished her capacity for productive resistance to policy changes to the call schedule. She may or may not be able to identify with the oft-used term *burnout,* characterized by feelings of energy depletion or exhaustion, increased mental distance from one's job, feelings of negativism or cynicism related to one's job, and reduced professional efficacy.[43] However, it is clear that life circumstances are affecting her work experience. Jody, like all of us, may be dealing with *spillover effects,* where the demands of one dimension of life (family) affect behavior in another dimension (work).[44]

Even if we don't look to burnout for explanations and tools for dealing with Jody's behavior, there is a good chance that she is experiencing low work-life integration, a probable precursor to burnout. Further evidence that this may be at play is a study showing that physicians who match Jody's demographics are most likely to have poor work-life integration. Namely, these are "women, single, aged 35 years or older, and who work more hours and call nights."[45]

Patient Dynamics

While patients have always come to their healthcare providers with expectations to be treated compassionately and competently, today, they are armed with more information about illnesses[46] and injuries as well as physician responsibilities. Additionally, the aging population comes with more complexity in diagnosing, treating, and coordinating care, all of which may take the physician out of their typical scope of practice.[47]

For many physicians like Jody, the changes in patient panels and interactions are among the reasons cited for decreased meaning in their work. We recognize that, in some cases, patient care can be used as a defensive shield meant to excuse bad behavior. When physicians are accused of being disruptive, the response that doing so in service of excellent patient care, safety, and quality often delays addressing the issue until those urgent issues are investigated.

Team Dynamics

Jody has never felt like she was part of the team. Further, we don't have reason to believe the team has been deliberately developed, with constructive norms, a shared sense of mission, and strong values that lead to psychological safety.[48] Now, when the team needs to come together and address a short-term staffing shortage, this lack of attention to team cohesiveness is causing division and resentment. If this is the case, how can the team possibly come together to hire someone who increases team effectiveness and cohesiveness?

The importance of *psychologically safe teams* — teams that function effectively and cohesively — is discussed in more depth later in the book. For now, we note that the physician leader, who is faced with the immediate issue of addressing Jody's disruptive behavior, can't prioritize team building. While a valid approach and one we recommend, it is not often realistic. Team interventions produce changes in individual behavior over the long term.

Nonetheless, if Amit is to engage with Jody effectively, he'll need to show her that he understands the added pressure of the rigid (and somewhat unforgiving) expectations espoused by her teammates, and the norm that makes it difficult for her to raise her concerns diplomatically. By doing so, Amit is not accepting excuses, he is providing an honest awareness of the team dynamics affecting Jody.

Leader Skill and Experience

In this case, the leader (Amit) is new and was promoted from within. While this approach to leader succession brings with it a deep understanding of the hospital and the community it serves, it is also likely that Amit hasn't had much time to develop his leadership skills. We would hope that he has considered the demands of his role intellectually and that he has observed his own leaders to determine how he'd like to proceed. But, until one steps into their first leadership role, it is difficult to know how to deliver on even the most well-thought-out intentions.

Harvard researcher Linda Hill recounts an illustrative quote about stepping into a leadership role for the first time in her classic 2007 article titled "Becoming the Boss." She writes: "It's the feeling you get when you have a child. On day X minus 1, you still don't have a child. On day X, all of a sudden, you're a mother or a father and you're supposed to know everything there is to know about taking care of a kid."[49]

In most healthcare environments, leadership also comes with peer-to-peer relationships and loyalties that are difficult to navigate. Some experts suggest that leaders distance themselves from peers[50] while strengthening relationships with other institutional leaders.[51] While it is ideal to prepare to lead peers years before one is called to do so,[52] it is often difficult to alter one's social contract with former peers fast enough to fully inhabit the role of the leader.

Even if they could, many leaders don't want to sacrifice barbeques, golf, or socializing with the families of peers in their practice. And, to the extent that strong social networks are one important way to manage the stress of making tough yet sound decisions — clinical and non-clinical — we don't know that we want them to abandon their social connections. In Chapter 11, we address a special consideration for physician leaders: dealing with target physicians who have been friends.

Considerable evidence shows that leaders tend to build strong relationships with a select group of followers — the proverbial *in-group*.[53] Members of this inner circle spend more time with the leader, have better access, communicate more often, and develop a deeper base of trust than do others within the follower ranks. Interestingly, being admitted into the in-group has little to do with work performance and more to do with the similarity of interests and values. In our example, it's easy to conclude that Jody is not in the inner circle.

Team Diversity

Diverse teams are increasingly common in healthcare, and we know that the way diverse teams are led affects their effectiveness. Diverse teams have more information available to solve problems and greater collective effort to execute their solutions. However, if not managed properly, leaders may fail to realize these benefits due to subgrouping and intergroup bias. As if new leaders weren't traveling multiple learning curves at once already, evidence-based recommendations for managing diverse teams recently became available.[54]

In any team, individual characteristics and demographic differences may have historically caused inequities and exclusivity that have not been adequately addressed, and the diversification of healthcare is not over. Add to the mix people with different credentials (like APPs), career paths, and training, and the goal of creating an inclusive environment becomes harder and more important than ever.

Further complicating things in our example, gender is a *salient* social group for Jody. She is the only woman in the practice, and, simply put, she stands out. Research on salience suggests that her behavior may receive more attention, and it is more likely that it is attributed to her gender.[55] This can create further distance between her and her colleagues, which undermines team effectiveness and may inhibit her ability to change her behavior.

Industry Trends

Changes in the healthcare landscape have profoundly affected the practice of medicine. Studies show that physicians are experiencing higher levels of burnout due to increased regulation and documentation requirements,[56] workloads, and reduced autonomy due to pressures associated with profitability.[57] As a result, many physicians experience disruptions to work-life integration[58] and mental health challenges (which are increasingly stigmatized[59,60]).

Some physicians may leave clinical care altogether. In fact, a 2023 study showed that 40.3% of physicians planned to reduce their clinical time within the next 12 months, which places further pressure on those who continue practicing.[59] Anecdotally, many practicing physicians we coach are hopeless about the return of meaning in their work unless they step into a leadership role where they will have some agency and influence.

But, as we'll see, agency and influence only go so far. In many cases, physician leaders are faced with the challenge of mitigating circumstances or optimizing outcomes. They are unable to control new reporting requirements, the hospital system's decreased reliance on locums to address staffing shortages, or the impact of a closed OR due to flooding. While physicians may ascend the leadership ladder or join their professional organization's advocacy efforts in order to increase their real or perceived influence, physician leaders are often mitigating negative circumstances on a daily basis.

Given the considerations noted above, we conclude that disruptive behavior presents a classic *wicked problem* — one that may have multiple causes and multiple solutions that must be evaluated from multiple perspectives.

Taking a systems view of the situation is the first step, but doing so may require a change in perspective on behalf of the physician leader. Specifically, physician leaders need to understand that pausing to consider the system-level issues before addressing the individual disruption doesn't implicitly excuse the behavior, nor does it absolve the physician leader from addressing it on behalf of patient care and safety, team effectiveness, or hospital functioning. In that pause, we encourage leaders to determine if their actions will be in service of (1) agency and authority, (2) influence, or (3) responsiveness to organizational realities and industry trends, which we'll call polarity management.

Agency and authority are direct. When physicians use their authority, they can set direction, make decisions, and enforce compliance. However, all this also implies a higher degree of certainty that leaders' actions will resolve the disruptive behavior than leaders likely have. Given the authority they have, the best place to exercise agency is in their personal approach to the situation. Physician leaders may use some agency and authority when deploying a disciplinary policy or creating a contract with the target physician, but its use should be limited in favor of influence.

In contrast to agency and authority, influence involves the ability to affect or shape someone's actions, behaviors, or opinions indirectly. Influence is more about persuasion, guidance, and inspiration rather than command and control. When leaders act in the realm of influence, they may not have the formal power to enforce outcomes, but they can shape decisions and actions through various means, such as communication, example-setting, or emotional appeal. In this way, influence can also build trust when it is exercised alongside understanding, conversation, and collaborative problem-solving.

Logically, physician leader interactions with target physicians are likely a blend of agency and influence. Yet, in the chapters to come, we recommend weighting influence more heavily. Activities that increase the functioning of the team overall are similarly an opportunity to influence rather than control behavior, and that influence must unfold over a longer period of time.

Responsiveness to largely external forces, such as organizational realities and industry trends, is best described as *polarity management*. In his book *Polarity Management*, Barry Johnson reminds us that "for every complex problem, there is a simple solution, and its wrong."[61]

Any external force or organizational practice is there for a reason. When the decision was made, it was a reasonable response to an issue the organization faced. But, as time goes on, the negative consequences of those responses become clear. As a leader, you begin to respond to the negative consequences in ways that resolve your individual issues, but in many cases, your response either reinforces the externality or creates a shift … that eventually starts to produce negative consequences as well.

Polarity management is more complex than agency or influence, so let's use our earlier example of Jody and Amit to make this clearer. As the physician leader, Amit (with the support of upper administration) has started to respond to demands from new hires for reduced call in their initial contracts, and that addresses, to some extent, the recruiting problem. But, over time, the practice employs fewer people to take call. Consequently, Amit feels better about asking veteran physicians to take it.

Now a veteran physician, Jody, is raising concerns. While Amit can't dismiss the *ways* she is raising concerns, he must take a minute to think through the consequences of the practice's management of the recruiting polarity. Placing all the blame at Jody's feet may make Amit feel as if he's solved the problem, but really, he's just continued to ignore the polarity.

Again, you may not have the authority to change the problem of having fewer physicians to cover a static call schedule, nor may you be able to influence it immediately. However, you can recognize it and consider systemic factors in Jody's circumstances when you address her disruptive behavior.

But, before we get too far ahead of ourselves in moving through the next steps with the target physician, a map is in order. Once physician leaders situate their circumstances within the map, they will be better able to determine the nature of their next steps. While we have revealed the complexity in determining the cause of the disruptive physician's behavior, the next steps shouldn't be complicated. Rather, they should be straightforward and matched to the pieces of the system you've chosen to address.

SYSTEMS THEORY

What we've been calling a "map" is an outcome of a systems-perspective, which has become a cornerstone of the organizational sciences. In organizational behavior, we think in terms of individual performers, their leaders, their teams, their locations or units, their organizations, and so on.[62-64]

For instance, the National Academy of Medicine (NAM) adopted a systems-view of physician well-being.[65] In it, they acknowledge the impact of factors such as society and culture, organizational factors, and regulations on individual clinician resilience. This multidimensional perspective is significant, given that resilience is often conceptualized as an individual trait that protects against burnout.

In short, the National Academy of Medicine is acknowledging what Christina Maslach noted in her 2001 article, "it is paradoxical that most interventions to alleviate burnout focus on individuals since the research suggests that situational and organizational factors play a bigger role in burnout."[66]

Just as the NAM has done with well-being, physician leaders need to adopt a framework that situates target physicians and their behaviors within a system in ways that help the leader address it. No matter the framework you adopt, remember that in nearly all cases, individual behaviors and responses in the workplace are a by-product of individual characteristics and their immediate and general environments.

Figure 1 presents the systems-level framework that guided our thinking throughout this book, and we provide some additional assistance in how to engage in agency, influence, and polarity management.

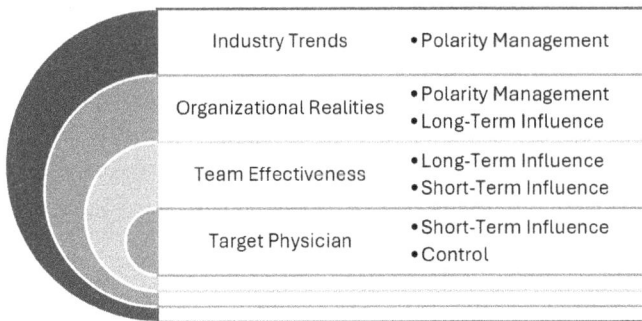

Industry Trends	• Polarity Management
Organizational Realities	• Polarity Management • Long-Term Influence
Team Effectiveness	• Long-Term Influence • Short-Term Influence
Target Physician	• Short-Term Influence • Control

FIGURE 1. Systems-Level Framework for Addressing Target Physicians

As you'll recognize, the target physician and their behavior are part of an interconnected system where a change or action by any part of the system has some impact (even if minor) on all other parts of the system. This concept of interrelatedness helps us recognize that target physician behavior does not occur in isolation.

It is conveniently tempting to assert that if we can create conditions to alter the behavior of a single problematic physician, everything will fall into place, and all will be well. However, the situation is likely to be more nuanced and complicated. While disruptive behaviors must be addressed, doing so within the context of the overall system may require special attention to a range of factors beyond a single target.

Once physician leaders understand the basics of the relevant system, they can choose the most appropriate response or approach. While we can't be certain of the exact route, we can be relatively sure that leaders will need to use a mix of approaches that will likely be at least somewhat aligned with the nature of the activities listed on the right-hand side of the diagram in Figure 1.

This is akin to planning a trip overseas: we know that we will use ground transportation on roads, but we could use any number of modes and roads to get to our destination. Likewise, the techniques leaders choose may influence the road taken and vice versa. At some point, leaders need to choose how to get across the water, which may result in a completely different set of techniques and routes. In planning any approach with the target physician, the leader's choice of technique and approach will vary.

When physician leaders *manage polarities*, they should strive for a more nuanced understanding of the reasons things are the way they are. Progress is almost always the result of a desire to solve a specific problem. In that regard, it may be appropriate to ask what problems industry trends or organizational realities solve in addition to the problems they may be creating.

Leaders should take care to keep the positive aspects of the trend or reality in place while addressing the negative aspects. In our example, this may mean taking another look at the contracts created with new partners and requiring more call or more flexibility to alleviate some of the pressure on physicians like Jody in the long term.

When leaders are *exercising influence*, they must realize that there can be a time lag between actions and effects. Over the longer term, leaders can advocate for an increase in the locums' budget or make a case for a nocturnal hospitalist to relieve call responsibilities for physicians in their area of responsibility. Likewise, if leaders are working with their team to create a stronger sense of identity, working agreements, and cohesion, these outcomes will require repetition and reinforcement to become embedded.

When working with the immediate team, there are some more immediate outcomes we can predict. Specifically, the attention and effort focused on team dynamics may make Jody's development easier for her (due to teammates' deeper understanding and cohesion) and may make Jody more open to feedback and behavior change (due to evidence that her leader, Amit, understands the systems-level issues). However, as experience teaches us, lasting change does not happen with one intervention.

Shorter-term influence also comes into play regarding the leader's interactions with the target physician. The next chapters go into much greater detail, but influencing lasting behavior changes is a result of the trust, commitment, and motivation of the target physician. Although leaders cannot control these factors, they can influence them by understanding the target physician's values and priorities, assuming good intent, engaging collaboratively, and taking 100% responsibility for 50% of the issue.

Leaders should use agency and authority only to the extent it is required by their role when dealing with the target physician. We recommend adhering to policy and holding the physician accountable when behavior warrants it. Few things are as disappointing to high performers as seeing low or problematic performers treated as equal contributors to the team and its culture. But, as we'll discuss, using authority sparingly will lead to deeper and more lasting professional improvement on the part of the target physician. On the other hand, we strongly recommend leaders use their own agency and use it wisely when it comes to their self-management throughout this process. In short, be responsive and avoid reactivity.

RESPOND; DON'T REACT.

"Respond, don't react" is a common action item for physicians who have been required to come to us for coaching as part of their performance improvement plan. Essentially, those leaders who have escalated this concern about the physician want them to pause and process their emotions before acting. This requires a tremendous amount of emotional intelligence on the part of the physician being coached, and it takes focused self-awareness before a pause can be built into their reaction to obstacles or misunderstandings. We will address these themes in more detail in a later chapter.

In Amit's case, one of the reasons he was promoted was his ability to respond (pause and process) before interacting with patients, fellow physicians, providers, and nurses. However, physician leadership requires that responsiveness be stretched to consider all the factors listed above and perhaps others that are artifacts of the leader's nuanced environment.

In some cases, that means the initial response toward the target physician shows empathy (e.g., "I know you have shouldered a lot of the non-specialized cases in our practice for several years now, and more call just gives you more broken bones and less opportunity to build your geriatric practice"). In other cases, that may mean rallying the team to create a better sense of camaraderie and shared goals.

Or, in still other cases, the disruptive behavior points to a narrow solution set (e.g., a disciplinary process that only allows one option for physician remediation) that needs to be interrogated. While the disruptive behavior on the part of the target physician should not be excused, the leader's ability to recognize that it is in response to perceived challenges (such as workload, in this case) that may be addressed with other solutions (such as locums or hospitalist coverage) is key to changing it.

SUMMARY CHECKLIST

- Disruptive behavior in physicians is complex and influenced by individual skills, personal circumstances, patient dynamics, team dynamics, leader skills, team diversity, and industry trends.
- A systems-level perspective is necessary to address such behavior effectively.
- When taking action, leaders must use a deliberate combination of agency and authority, influence, and management of external forces.
- Consider all aspects of the target physician's behavior:
  - What are their overall circumstances like? Have they changed? How is this physician doing when it comes to burnout, loneliness, and social support?
  - If not part of the reason the issue came to your attention, understand the impact on the team. Then, consider how the team is influencing the target physician's behavior.
  - Even if leaders cannot change target physicians, are there organizational or industry-level issues that also need to be recognized? Having an awareness of them positions leaders for more trust-building with the target physician.
- Notwithstanding issues that need to be addressed immediately (like the target physician's behavior disrupting patient care, safety, or experience), pause and reflect. Call on mentors for advice. Identify the long-term goals you have for your team and your organization and prepare to act in alignment with that vision.
- We encourage physician leaders to invest in their own leadership, using this opportunity to build skills in using authority, influence, and polarity management so they are better equipped to handle situations that arise in the future.

CHAPTER 4

Are They Really That Different?

....

Let's revisit our conversation with Dave, the orthopedic surgeon introduced in Chapter 1, who was a perfectionist with a caustic tone. During our second meeting, Dave asserted, "OK, I can get fired up. But I've seen other doctors, far more senior doctors, say and do things worse than me. They get a pass, and I get sent for help."

We reminded Dave of the broader systemic themes consistent with those mentioned in Chapter 3. For example, the surgeons to whom he referred had been with the practice for many years, building rapport and understanding with colleagues and staff. Perhaps an occasional harsh statement was being evaluated within an overall climate of support. Dave was unmoved. "All I know is that my behaviors don't differ that much from others." Dave's point was valid, raising an important question: Are target physicians significantly different from their peers? A bit of a conundrum. The answer, typically, is both yes and no.

It is easy to assume that target physicians are deviants who, in terms of personality and behaviors, stray widely from the norm. These assumptions are understandable. Physicians who engage in chronic disruptive behaviors complicate your role as a physician leader and, as such, complicate your life. They erode the morale of your unit, diminishing the drive and commitment that are essential for peak performance and employee satisfaction.

Amid the chaotic tension that target physicians have created, they often remain unaware and unconcerned. They forge ahead — at times obliquely — convinced that they are the only members of the band who are marching in step. It's easy to dislike and subtly demonize these troubled souls. And this is the honest awareness from which physician leaders must start and from which they must emerge.

Hard as it may be, we encourage physician leaders to focus not on the damage being done but on the target physician as a *person* — a person who needs support, even as they at times appear to dismiss and shun any help that is offered. As such, we encourage leaders to strive for the high road, even as that principled intention is challenged. Amid these concerns, we begin with a view of individual motivation guided by the research and theory on individual motivation and change.

Physician leaders must try to understand why the target person is being difficult and problematic — a challenge much more intense than it may appear.[67] Understanding individual motivation is complex and multivariate. Certainly, personality plays a role. Background and experience are also factors. Personal goals and aspirations come into play. Indeed, trying to understand why target physicians behave problematically is a noble and somewhat unattainable search. Yet, we encourage leaders to try to understand why these problematic people do what they do.

Frustrating as they may be, in most cases, target physicians are more alike than dissimilar from the rest of the leader's physician base. Admittedly, target physician behaviors are extreme, differentiating their characteristics and preferences from those that typify most physicians. Further, for many target physicians, these behaviors play out with little sensitivity and finesse.

Given these perspectives, it's important to resist the "us against them" thinking that can emerge. Instead, we encourage leaders to consider target physicians as team members who need special attention, structured guidance, clear and reasonable guardrails, and ongoing support. Target physicians are problematic, but they are not pariahs. A deeper understanding of the nature and characteristics of physicians who exhibit disruptive behaviors can be helpful. With this preamble, let's examine the data.

PHYSICIAN CHARACTERISTICS

In the following section, we consider some of the prevalent characteristics of the physicians on the leader's team. Let's begin with some obvious factors. As a group, physicians are highly educated, highly intelligent, and highly competent in their specialized areas of training and practice. While variations exist across the physician population, these underlying dimensions are unassailable. Logically, of course, training, intelligence, and clinical competencies are essential for attaining the highest levels of patient outcomes and clinical success.

However, intelligence and competence may come with their own set of demons. Here, concerns arise when one of three outcomes appears. First, highly intelligent people may place minimal reliance on others, preferring instead to draw on their own insights and analytic skills to address issues that arise. Second, there may be a tendency to under-communicate by limiting explanatory communications directed toward others. This occurs because a course of action that appears cloudy and uncertain to others is readily apparent to the physician. Third, competence and intelligence may lead to perfectionist tendencies — a preference that can be commendable but also interpersonally off-putting and stress-inducing.[68] Weaving the line between high-quality standards and perfectionism is a tenuous walk.

Additionally, physicians tend to be quick studies, especially within the realm of their specialty and expertise. Through training and practice, physicians process complex issues, evaluate data, make informed decisions, and move to actions that they gauge to have the best probability of success. Within this process, when additional data or evidence become relevant, decision calculations are reworked, and subsequent, data-based decisions are enacted. In short, physicians are *clinically decisive*, able to present viable plans of action even when complete and conclusive data are lacking.[69]

In general, clinical teams expect physician decisiveness to be a factor that promotes quality clinical outcomes. However, when a quick study is combined with under-communication and perfectionist biases, others (especially staff) can feel left behind, leading to a potential breach in a team-oriented culture. These concerns are exacerbated as we recognize that physicians tend to be tenacious and persistent in their clinical endeavors. In popular jargon, they display "grit" — perseverance and resilience, even in the face of adversity and setbacks.[70]

Physicians tend to have a high need to achieve, characterized by high personal and professional standards. Consistent with research on high achievers, physicians prefer to affect matters that face them rather than leave outcomes to luck, fate, chance, or the decisions made by those with less direct competence and credibility.[71]

Further, frustration ensues when structured goals of achievement are blunted by others' actions or inactions.[72] Some physicians handle this frustration with sensitivity, taking a genuine teaching and developmental approach toward others. However, some physicians (our target physicians) have yet to learn how to maintain standards of excellence while extending understanding and grace toward others.[73]

Closely related is an additional characteristic physicians generally possess: the need to avoid failure.[74] Given the need for achievement and the need to avoid failure, it is easy to understand how intense demands for excellence can manifest. At times, perceived inflexibility may be an outcome.

An additional combination of factors must be noted — factors that present as challenges for contemporary and emerging healthcare settings. Physicians have strong preferences and needs for autonomy and control. In fact, one of the frustrations physicians note is that their expectations and needs for autonomy and control are increasingly thwarted by large, complex, and bureaucratic organizational systems.

This becomes especially frustrating when physicians feel that important clinical decisions are compromised by those making broad strategic and financial decisions with insufficient regard for clinical and patient-centered needs. Accordingly, it is not surprising that many physicians rail against efforts that they perceive as diminishing their realm of desired independence.[75]

As noted in earlier chapters, we must emphasize a final factor or outcome confronting all physicians. Compared to the general population, physicians experience higher levels of depression and burnout. In fact, the Centers for Disease Control and Prevention (CDC) notes crisis levels of burnout among healthcare workers, indicating that the realm of burnout extends beyond physicians.[76] Here, there is an unfortunate differentiator. Despite the levels of stress that physicians experience, they often feel stigmatized for reaching out for help.[76]

PHYSICIANS AND DISRUPTIVE BEHAVIOR: A DARKER SIDE

Just as physicians are complex and multidimensional, those who exhibit chronic disruptive behaviors are understandably idiosyncratic. Here, however, research suggests common factors that are important for our consideration.

As noted above, physicians, in general, want and need control. In many ways, this preference coincides with the demands of the profession, where physicians are the ultimate clinical decision-makers regarding patient-centered clinical choices. However, physicians who display chronic disruptive behaviors typically have an especially strong need for control, and they often attempt to exert control over others through intimidating and dismissive behaviors.[77]

Note that our concern is not the *need* for control — an understandable demand of the profession. Rather, our focus is on the attendant variables: intimidation toward and dismissiveness of others. These disruptive behaviors strip others of their need to feel that they are people of significance, team members who make meaningful and impactful contributions. As such, control is not the central concern. *The diminishing approach to exerting desired control* is the issue.

The themes here are exacerbated when we recognize that target physicians often have an overly inflated ego and sense of self-worth — self-perceived images that can lead them to overestimate their abilities and underestimate or diminish the abilities of others with whom they work.[78]

Consistent with this overly skewed sense of confidence can be a tendency toward impulsive behavior, coupled with a limited capacity to listen to others and accept advice.[79,80] It's important to keep these themes in mind, as they represent a research-based behavioral backdrop for physician leaders choosing to address the disruptive behaviors of their target physicians.

Additionally, target physicians' view of how their behavior affects others is often distorted.[81] What they may perceive as "no big deal" may have a dramatic impact on others, especially those with lesser status and professional power. Consistent with these themes, target physicians dislike being questioned by others and, for the most part, are not receptive to criticism.[82] Of course, these tendencies complicate the work of physician leaders who attempt to provide guidance and help.

There is evidence that physicians who engage in chronic disruptive behavior may have unique personality and psychological dynamics, with at least one study reporting abnormal personality profiles among such physicians.[83] Further, those exhibiting chronic disruptive behaviors have been associated with low sociability, low personal trust, low personal contentment, and low emotional intelligence.[21,84] For some, their behavior is confounded by psychological disorders and complicated by chemical dependence.[85] Evidence suggests that substance abuse is likely to be present in at least 10% of cases.[85]

Common among the personality disorders that may also be present are paranoia (manifested by distrust of others and suspiciousness of others' intentions and motivations), narcissism (manifested by grandiosity and a need for admiration), low empathy, and passive-aggressiveness.[86] While we are careful with labels and stereotypes, it is prudent to understand the dynamics that research has indicated may be at play. Such a search for understanding enhances the sensitivity and empathy of physician leaders toward their target physicians.

The matter of narcissism demands a closer look. Research confirms that target physicians often display narcissistic personality characteristics.[24]

Originally conceived from Greek mythology, we generally think of narcissists as having strong self-centeredness, high levels of egocentrism, and excessive vanity.[87] But, we concur with research noting that for some roles (physicians would be one), a solid dose of narcissism can be essential to success.[88]

Here, it is helpful to consider a distinction proposed by Daniel Goleman: the distinction between *healthy narcissism* and *unhealthy narcissism*.[89] Healthy narcissism correlates with self-confidence and the ability to push on and thrive when confronting adversity and challenges. Indeed, such reflective confidence and tenacity are linked to overall success.

However, those displaying unhealthy narcissism exhibit seven characteristics (or at least some of these characteristics). These are: (1) a craving to be loved and adored by others; (2) a need for constant praise and affirmation; (3) an internal drive to achieve that is largely motivated by the personal glory it brings; (4) a tendency to pursue goals aggressively with little regard for how others are affected; (5) a reluctant and closed approach to criticism; (6) a tendency to view any form of criticism as a personal attack; and (7) a desire to exclude messages that fail to confirm success and greatness.[89]

Goleman offers another helpful commentary: "Whether a narcissist is healthy or unhealthy can be gauged by their capacity for empathy. The more impaired the person's ability to consider others, the less healthy is their narcissism."[89p.119]

Goleman's insight suggests that helping the unhealthy narcissist may hinge on the concept of empathy, an important component of emotional intelligence. Even without the narcissism label (or diagnosis), low emotional intelligence in general and diminished self-awareness and empathy in particular are perhaps the most critical characteristics of physicians who display disruptive behaviors.

One definition of emotional intelligence is "the set of abilities (verbal and nonverbal) that enable a person to generate, recognize, express, understand, and evaluate their own and others' emotions in order to guide that successfully cope with environmental demands and actions."[90p.72] The significance of diminished capacity in the arena of emotional intelligence is clear.[90]

As we progress to Section Two of this book, we will discuss ways that you, as a physician leader, can help target physicians build and use their personal emotional intelligence. Specifically, in Chapter 8, we discuss how to coach target physicians through common issues they may be facing using emotional intelligence as a frame.

FACING REALITY

Before ending this chapter, let's reset our perspective and intention. This book is written for you, the physician leader who is faced with a complex challenge. Perspective is important. Leaders confront target physicians who are, first and foremost, talented physicians — physicians who typically care deeply about their patients and who generally possess solid clinical skills.

However, target physicians have veered off-track, edging into patterns of chronic disruptive behaviors that may threaten patient well-being, staff morale, expectations of equity and fairness, and the overall cultural spirit that progressive clinical units desire to build and maintain.

Rather than tolerating or ignoring these distressed target physicians, we argue for and urge leaders to consider interventions. In general, these interventions are best when enacted earlier rather than later. Throughout this book, we help physician leaders develop a deeper understanding of their target physicians, avoid destructive labels, and take necessary interventional actions to address the myriad challenges they bring to the practice. The impact will be palpable.

AND OF COURSE … CONTEXT MAKES A DIFFERENCE

Behavior is designated as disruptive when it is inappropriate and unacceptable within a specific team or organizational context. Of course, the realm of acceptable behavioral norms can vary widely, especially when individual experiences span several clinical settings. For example, Dave (from Chapter 1) asserted that his aggressive style (and colorful language) was part of the norm during his residency and that he was doing nothing different from what he had normally done. However, Dave's style was outside the norm for his current team, which led to conflicts and complaints.

We encountered a similar matter with Lana. She worked five years at a clinic in another state before accepting her new role at a growing clinic in a mid-sized community. As she relayed to us, her previous team openly confronted and challenged one another in an effort for continuous improvement in serving patients. When Lana challenged others openly and somewhat unfiltered with her new team, colleagues were offended and defensively dismissed her debate-everything style.

The first task for the physician leader who is engaging a target physician is to carefully delineate what is acceptable and unacceptable within the current context. This is part of clarifying *shared values* and providing *crystal clear behavioral expectations* — activities that are fundamental for successful leadership.[91]

It is also important to help target physicians recognize that behavior that is accepted in a unique setting (say, when conducting surgery in the OR) may be unacceptable in other settings (when working on care teams with colleagues). Here, we encourage you to help establish the power of *switching behaviors* as situational demands change.

SUMMARY CHECKLIST

- Focus on the person first and try to understand why the target physician is displaying unacceptable/disruptive behavior.
- Resist "us versus them" thinking. Remember, target physicians are problematic, but they should not be demonized.
- Recognize that target physicians have a deep need for control. Further, they may exert control over others through intimidating and dismissive behaviors. Leaders are unlikely to affect the need for control; therefore, they should focus on eliminating the actions perceived to be intimidating and dismissive.
- Help target physicians understand the situational nature of their behaviors and encourage them to be cognizant of and practice switching (alternative) behaviors.
- Clarify the desired core values for your unit.
- Present clear expectations regarding behaviors deemed appropriate and necessary. There is no better starting point than establishing crystal clear expectations.

CHAPTER 5

Preparing to Engage with Your Target Physician

....

IN EARLIER CHAPTERS, we discussed the need to work with physicians who are displaying chronic distressed or disruptive behaviors. We noted the problematic nature of avoiding tough conversations and the debilitating and cumulative impact of an attitude of tolerance. Further, we emphasized the importance of early intervention, especially when the risks of escalation and labeling are high.

In this chapter, we focus on physician leaders as they prepare for their first interventions with the target physician. Several excellent sources are available that offer guidance for having difficult discussions with problematic people.[92-96] We will draw from these and other sources as we offer special applications for our physician audience.

One behavioral adage notes that *we hire a whole person*. The statement is profound in its simplicity and has an array of applications. When we employ a physician, we look for the right combination of skills, talents, and experiences to meet specific clinical needs and demands. But we get much more. We get unique personalities and jagged edges. We get personal problems, family dynamics, health issues, and quirks of temperament.

What we want and what we get cannot be segregated. Dimensions of life such as work and family spill over and affect one another.[97] Complicated and less than ideal, this is the behavioral landscape within which all leaders must work. And, as leaders do so — hopefully with respect and grace — they affect the tone or mood of the entire practice.[98]

PHYSICIAN LEADERS AS COACHES

Although executive coaching has received considerable attention during the past two decades, it is not our intention to encourage you to train as professional coaches. We recognize that you are busy with your clinical and administrative roles. Yet, successful leaders must engage in ongoing, supportive, and interactive communication that closely mirrors what has become known as coaching. Indeed, when physician leaders intervene and interact with target physicians in developmental exchanges, they are engaging in the process of managerial coaching.[99] We hope to help you navigate this new coaching terrain to achieve successful outcomes.

Although coaching is rooted in psychotherapy and psychology, managerial coaching emphasizes the work context.[100] Stated succinctly, managerial coaching is an exchange designed to enhance skills, competence, and overall performance.[101] When done best, managerial coaching is an ongoing relationship geared toward the development and growth of target physicians.

Ideally, this exchange is based on helping and supporting a target physician with a focus on positive behavioral change. Indeed, projecting the desire to help and support the target physician is one of the more critical elements for building successful developmental interactions, as we will discuss more fully below.

Original research and summaries from the Center for Creative Leadership suggest that coaching can enhance the performance of target physicians in at least five ways: (1) providing greater self-awareness; (2) providing greater and more complete understanding of the organizational and interpersonal contexts they confront; (3) improving critical thinking skills; (4) providing greater understanding of others; and (5) enhancing communication skills and capacity.[102,103] It is likely that leaders will be emphasizing one or more of these dimensions as they work with target physicians.

In general, physicians displaying disruptive behaviors are more open and receptive to coaching than to other forms of remedial actions (especially therapy).[104] Their willingness to engage in coaching is further enhanced when they believe that their physician leader is providing support and positive developmental activities geared to help the target physician.[105]

This support is best conveyed when it is legitimate and authentic. In other words, leaders should strive to orient their thinking toward a perspective of support and help. Such a mindset can be difficult, especially when target physicians create so many issues and concerns that disrupt others, consume the leader's time, and shift the leader's focus from more progressive and future-directed endeavors. Keep in mind that developing even the most challenging staff members is a key role for difference-making leaders.[106]

An additional point is important for physician leaders who engage in coaching to understand. Coaching conversations need not be overly time-consuming. In fact, relatively brief 20- or 30-minute exchanges can be quite productive. Coaching effectiveness is not predicated on the length of the encounter; rather, effectiveness derives from the strength of the coaching relationship, the authenticity and skills of the coach, and a commitment to the continuity of meetings.[107]

BUILDING A COACHING RELATIONSHIP

Successful coaching begins with the physician leader and the value framework they establish prior to any direct interaction. We know that working with physicians who exhibit chronic disruptive behaviors is complex and taxing, but it is also critical. Here, we offer four foundations for leaders to consider.

First, as noted above, coaching is a *relationship* — a theme that we will develop and refine throughout our writing. Relationships are neither casual exchanges nor passive interactions. Rather, relationships imply a depth of understanding, consideration, and concern. They imply talking and working together to achieve better outcomes. They are fortified by trust, the "intention to accept vulnerability based upon positive expectations of the intentions or behavior of another."[108]

Perhaps most fundamental, relationships imply continuity — ongoing exchanges between parties who truly care about collaboration and growth. There is general agreement that the nature and quality of the coaching relationship are the most critical factors in securing meaningful and successful coaching outcomes.[109]

Second, the fundamental purpose of the relationship is to *provide assistance* for the target physician who is being coached. It is important to realize that the immediate purpose of coaching is not to enhance the achievement of organizational goals, although such secondary outcomes are certainly desired. Rather, the immediate focus must be on the person: the physician who is being coached.

Assistance can, at times, take a rather circuitous route. Often, issues of personal significance, confidence, interpersonal anxieties, and a closed system of thinking about others must be addressed before any eventual performance and behavioral improvements have a chance of being markedly enhanced.

The third factor is an offshoot of the previous two. Here, we encourage leaders to project an *attitude of support* — part of broader themes known as *perceived organizational support* (POS) and *perceived supervisory support* (PSS). POS and PSS are perceptions that the organization and its leaders value the contributions of their employees, care about their employees, and are concerned with employee well-being.[110] Perceived support is related to several positive outcomes, including organizational commitment, job satisfaction, and enhanced desire to work for organizational success.[111] Not surprisingly, the most dramatic impacts arise when the support comes from one's immediate supervisor — in our case, the physician leader.[111]

Our fourth dimension of coaching pervades all others. Coaching is a *developmental process*. Here, to understand the arc of the coaching relationship, we must have some understanding of adult development and how developmental goals can be best achieved.[106] In general, developmental progress is not linear; rather, it involves a series of advances, plateaus, and even regressive backsliding as old and habitual behaviors flare under the heat of stressful situations. Here, leaders can help target physicians recognize that occasional stumbles are natural and even productive, given that awareness, learning, and future intentions are modified. An example may be helpful.

When we started to work with Jamie, our immediate points-of-entry were the three explosive exchanges he had with two nurses and a physician assistant in the preceding month. Working with Jamie over the next few months, we seemed to be making progress — that is, until a message popped up on our phones that bluntly asserted, "Well, I did it again. Can we talk?"

Jamie, responding to what he felt was a PA's lazy and clumsy response to a patient, had angrily lashed out at her once again. However, as we unpacked the episode, evidence of Jamie's growth was evident. Yes, he had exploded again; however, he immediately recognized his stumble, was aware of the precipitating events that had contributed to his frustration, had a keen sense of these *emotional triggers*, and even had a plan of action for learning from the event and moving ahead. And, perhaps most important, Jamie had already extended an apology.

None of these elements of reflective self-awareness and action would have occurred before our coaching time together. Importantly, Jamie recognized that while he had stumbled, he had not failed. Further, we were able to once again discuss how to hold the PA to high clinical expectations without going "over the top." As we reminded Jamie, we are all works in progress.

Let's take the next step to help you, as physician leaders, prepare for your developmental coaching interactions. We encourage you to consciously adapt "the coach's mindset" discussed below.

THE COACH'S MINDSET

When you coach, it is important to orient yourself prior to each meeting by centering on the coach's mindset. Let us explain.

The coaching exchange — the entire exchange — is not about you. Rather, the focus must be on helping target physicians reach their potential, become better versions of themselves, and become more positive contributors to the overall team.

Whatever the precipitating factors, leaders should begin by attempting to understand and meet the target physicians where they are. Remember that every physician is a complicated and independent person. Each physician brings a unique set of needs, goals, passions, expectations, and fears. Each comes with their own defensive armor, honed over the years to protect the character, ego, and significance of its holder.

It is easy for a physician leader who is taking on a coaching role to be thrown off-target by prickly or undesired target physician mannerisms. In one of our coaching relationships, the client refused to make eye contact during our first session as she pressed and challenged us with largely unanswerable questions. In another situation, the client was so haughty and dismissive that we fought growing feelings of dislike. In another situation, the client was so ramblingly unfocused that following and charting the seemingly random comments created a stream-of-consciousness quagmire.

Yet, in each of these situations, we were able to create helpful and successful outcomes. How? Although there is no magic formula, the six themes below should be helpful.

First, remind yourself that the target physician is a special, idiosyncratic individual with a unique personality and set of behaviors. You likely are keenly aware of which behaviors are helping and which are hurting the target physician's progress; however, allow the physician latitude to grow in their own way rather than merely conforming to your assessments and prescriptions. Regardless of what happens during the interactions, maintain a posture of deep respect toward the target physician. This can, at times, be easier said than done.

One client pushed us to respond to scenarios that had brought her less-than-desired outcomes. She would describe the situation and then combatively demand that we prescribe how "we would have handled it." We tried to ask her to look at her actions and dissect the parts that worked and those that did not. She would have no part of it. "No, what would *you* do?" She was challenging us and testing our credibility to judge if we were worthy of her trust. We sensed the need to move in a different direction.

Our response: "We were not there, and we have limited capacity to evaluate the emotions and intensity of the situation. We also do not know the characters involved or the history among participants that always adds to the mix. But we do know this. The situation is primed to explode. Your comments, whether justified or not, were sure to be taken defensively and argumentatively by your colleagues. The context begged for patience, calmness, letting your colleagues know they have been heard, and affirming that you understand what they are feeling. So, we would try to do that, which would be hard, given that we'd probably be angry that we were challenged in such a public way."

She said nothing, but after the opening session, she stopped pushing. A different tone emerged. She became more self-reflective and began to answer the questions she had previously posed to us. Importantly, she allowed herself to share with us some deeper personal revelations that helped us move ahead in a real and meaningful way. Through the processes together, we had progressed from "superficial" to "relevant," but it came through a process.

Second, exercise patience and allow yourself to be surprised by the target physician. As a physician leader, you like to have things figured out. It allows you to exercise a degree of control. In your time-sensitive world, you want answers and solutions, and you need them to occur quickly.

However, coaching is a process that demands a more subtle approach. Allow yourself the patience of being on the edge, not fully in control, but ready to roll with the next twist that comes along. As such, your coaching relationship is a "living" relationship that evolves through deeper levels of complexity and understanding.

Third, approach your coaching meetings as a scanner, as a truth-teller, as a summarizer, and as a reflector — skills born of careful listening and probing questioning. For example, we listened for nearly 30 minutes as one client emoted about what had happened that very day — a microcosm, she asserted, of what went on all the time.

When she was exhausted and came up for air, we took a brief turn. "We are hearing three main points. First, you feel you must prove, over and over again, how good you are. Second, you feel that you are out of step — more serious and work-focused — than your peers and even your boss."

We stopped and asked if all this seemed accurate, and she assured us that it was spot-on. We continued: "But third, and most critical, you feel unappreciated — unappreciated for all you do and all you contribute. And it's not fair. And it hurts. You receive little affirmation. And you feel somewhat insignificant despite all the work you do and all the accomplishments you provide."

We recognized that she was struggling to maintain composure. And as such, our fourth relational foundation came in. *In coaching, less is often more.* She needed to absorb the three previous points. And she needed a base of affirmation. "What you are feeling is natural and reasonable. It's what we all feel and need. Significance is a powerful motivator, perhaps our most powerful. To desire that affirmation, that confirmation, that approval that you are important and significant is natural. It is why we work."

Here, leaders are encouraged to *focus*. Eschew the laundry list of corrective options. Instead, concentrate on one or two changes that will truly make a difference, even if they are simply changes in self-awareness. Through this process, progress incrementally.[112]

Our fifth point concerns relationships. All physician leaders who engage in coaching actions want to make a difference and help a target physician push forward to surmount an otherwise unsurmountable mountain. We want target physicians to have a transformational impact on our clients and their work lives.

Let's step back for a moment, as a caveat is in order. We believe this transformational perspective is ill-advised. In fact, it's usually a dangerous overreach to seek a transformation — some new person, new identity, or metamorphosis for our target physicians.

Instead, seek a *transition*. This involves trying out some new ideas, thoughts, behaviors, and approaches. We grow and progress incrementally, and we do so through a series of ebbs and flows — a decidedly non-linear process. As a physician who is engaged in coaching, your goal is not and should not be to "change" people's personalities — an almost impossible task.

Instead, your goal is to help the target physician gain additional skills and learn how to *flex* beyond their preferred and habitual styles when the situation dictates that such a shift is useful. This skill of *flexing behaviors* is so important that we will delve into it further in the next chapter. Again, your goal should be to help the physician feel comfortable with who they are while growing, expanding, and flexing their skills, perspectives, and approaches.

Our sixth foundation is this: *It is almost always easier to start doing something than it is to stop doing something.* We worked with a surgeon whose perceived arrogance and dismissiveness drove the nurses who worked with him to a regular barrage of complaints. When asked what he did, the surgeon professed that he really didn't know. But he added, "There must be something I need to stop doing." Perhaps. However, we suggested that it was hard to stop doing something that had become such an ingrained part of his routine that he was not really sure what specific behaviors were problematic.

After assuring that he did not yell, swear, berate, or engage in other aggressively destructive behaviors, we changed course. "We'd like to suggest that you do one small thing that you are not currently doing. We want you to address each nurse and technician by name and simply thank them and affirm their part in making the clinical procedure successful. Nothing over the top. It may be this simple … 'Jane, this was a complicated surgery. Thanks for all you did. It really made a difference.'"

As the surgeon applied this new behavior, we discussed its impact. At first, nothing was discernable; yet, over the next few months, he reported a much more open and authentic relationship with staff.

In summary, physician leaders are working to help their physicians gain perspective. Leaders are helping physicians see themselves as others see them by gauging and processing the impressions others have built. It's tricky here. The target physician who describes his behavior under stress as "firm and decisive" may be unaware that his staff perceives those same behaviors as "angry and dismissive." The impressions that others have of us offer key insight.

Try not to argue with the target physician, as it is generally a fruitless activity that produces little more than natural defensiveness. Instead, pursue a slightly different tact. "I'm not saying that you are angry and dismissive. I am suggesting that these are the perceptions, the impressions that others draw when they encounter you under highly stressful situations." This distinction, while subtle, is critical.

THE COACH'S SELF-AWARENESS AND PERSPECTIVE-TAKING

Adopting the aforementioned foundational viewpoints and mindsets is important, but it is also critical for physician leaders to understand their own values, emotional triggers, and behavioral tendencies as they engage with their target physicians. Here, physician leaders should be clear on their core values and understand that any negative emotions they may be feeling as they relate to the target physician are likely a signpost for those values.

As Susan David suggests in her work on emotional agility,[113] emotions can get us *hooked*. When we try to minimize them, they seem to become stronger, sometimes influencing the coaching conversation we are entering.

Instead of trying to suppress emotions, we recommend getting clear on the values they are pointing us to and responding from that foothold rather than the unfocused and unstable platform of emotions.

For example, we worked with a physician leader who was about to enter a conversation about a physician's failure to uphold his commitments to his partners to absorb the patient panel of a retiring physician until a replacement could be found. In preparing him for the interaction, we suggested he think through the venue, the opening line, and the behavioral request.

We had been working with this leader on acknowledging his emotions at work, so we were delighted when, as we talked, he stopped suddenly. "You know what? I'm angry with him. Not because he failed to live up to expectations but because I've bent over backward to make his life easier time and time again. And this is the thanks I get? I'm using valuable time with my coach to plan the details of this meeting."

As we talked further, we identified that the leader's values of equity and fairness were at play, as was his strongly held belief that while he was in a formal leadership position, he was part of a team. These values were being challenged by his need to address this physician's careless behavior.

Once the leader identified his emotion (anger) and its associated value and shifted his reason for the emotion, it melted away. The details became less important than his guiding principles for the meeting, which became his first comment and the only thing he prepared: "I am frustrated to have to bring this to your attention, given that I have always invested in your success and all of us are important to the success of our practice."

Getting clear on your values may also open your aperture more widely when listening to target physicians describe their perspective of the situation. If you listen carefully, you can discern the values of others, which may help you stabilize emotional conversations while providing an additional resource that may help change behavior.

Most often, target physicians give clues as to why they act the way they do: the patient deserves excellence (i.e., patient care); scheduling the OR has become unnecessarily difficult (i.e., efficiency); or the staff doesn't understand (i.e., competence and/or status). Naming these values as they surface and inquiring about them in ways that help the physician see how they, as leaders, can lean into them while they develop may be an effective approach.

Second, physician leaders should make sure they have created the circumstances necessary for their feedback to be well received. This involves taking the perspective of target physicians, even if their perspective may not be the one that leaders currently hold. It may also involve owning one's contribution to the negative performance.[114] For example, were expectations clear? Has the situation gone unaddressed for some time, such that the target physicians may feel as though nothing was problematic about their approach? Has the leader failed to deliver on a resource that was intended to mitigate the negative behavior? Owning one's part in the performance breakdown will be an important step to soften the inevitable initial response to broaching the first performance conversation.

Feedback, particularly improvement-focused feedback, doesn't feel good. It challenges physicians' sense of identity and competence, and the immediate reaction is often a way to defend against those threats. To prepare for the conversation, physician leaders should understand that this is going to make the target physician feel vulnerable and threatened, even if their response is angry, defensive, or an attempt to deflect blame. Ensuring that the target leader knows that the physician leader empathizes with the difficulty of acknowledging performance feedback (let alone using it to make positive change) may soften the initial reaction, build trust, and set the stage for more rapid performance improvement.

To a large extent, in this section, we are focusing on the emotional self-awareness of physician leaders. Emotional self-awareness is the foundation of emotional and social intelligence, and it has special significance for your coaching conversations.[89]

Realistically, the target physician has added complexity to the leader's role; they have affected the team and have demanded an inordinate amount of your time. You now must engage in developmental coaching exchanges, taking more time and perhaps stretching the target physician's range of interpersonal skills and comfort. Accordingly, it is reasonable to expect some degree of negative affect toward the target person. As we have discussed, admitting this reality and putting these emotions into constructive focus are important as leaders ponder developmental conversations.

An example may be helpful. A few years ago, we were asked to work with Ben, a manager who was having trouble connecting with and leading others. We knew Ben from his participation in a six-month workshop that we had led. We found Ben to be confrontational, relishing his self-described role as a contrarian who challenged the *status quo*. We considered him haughty and even pugnacious. He aggressively challenged his colleagues during discussions and seemed to enjoy pushing us, even on rather inconsequential points. Truth be told, we hesitated to work with Ben because, well, we just did not like this guy very much. Indeed, Ben made it easy to dislike him.

In thinking through the situation and our possible work together, two themes kept emerging. First, Ben was extremely smart and had excellent ideas. Second, Ben seemed to have no idea how to disagree without being disagreeable. After due consideration and ample self-talk, we accepted the challenge. Although far from smooth, we were able to make progress, and Ben secured a new leadership role that he desired.

Our first step was to confront our feelings and emotions regarding Ben and his behaviors, reminding us to take the higher ground and not let Ben's jabs and barbs get under our skin. Further, we were able to establish a bit of a game plan, providing Ben with some freedom, checking our emotional arousal, and setting a few guidelines that would promote progress. In short, by honestly connecting with our emotions, we were able to encounter Ben with a more positive and supportive attitude.

There is gold here. You do not have to like everyone with whom you work. Talent prevails, and it comes in various shades of personality and behavior. Getting yourself emotionally attuned for the upcoming conversation helps ameliorate the natural tendency to "take the bait" that those with troublesome behaviors often toss into the conversational waters.

Leaders often are aware of certain actions that target physicians use to get under others' skin. Awareness of these "triggers" can help leaders recognize them and check their responses during developmental conversations.

BALANCING DEVELOPMENT AND ACTION

There is broad agreement among most experts that successful coaches are not problem-solvers; rather, they are facilitators.[115] Problem-solvers deal with immediate issues and seek timely resolutions. Facilitators focus on development. Facilitators want others to gain understanding and insight. They want to help others learn how to unpack situations and arrive at sound answers. Facilitators help others develop an approach to complex situations and events.

Facilitation is a paced process that helps others assess situations, consider relevant inquiries, gather necessary information, gain assurance, and move forward with confidence and conviction. In many ways, facilitators are teachers.

With regard to the situations we are discussing in this book, we suggest a slight twist. Your role as a physician leader who is helping a physician colleague with chronic disruptive patterns is complex and fundamentally different. *Essentially, you must be both a sensitive developmental facilitator and a facilitator who ensures that problematic behavior is remediated.* Straddling both dimensions is necessitated by the disruptive nature of the situation and the impact that it has on your team and your desired culture. The chapters that follow are framed by this dual focus.

SUMMARY CHECKLIST

- Keep in mind that we employ a whole person — talent comes with complications.
- Embrace your role to engage in developmental coaching — interactions that are especially important for our target physicians.
- Build a respectful relationship between you and your target physician. Strive to provide help, offer support, and foster development.
- Recognize your personal values, emotional triggers, and existing negative feelings toward the target physician.

Conversations and Action Steps

CHAPTER 6

The Conversation

....

I N THE FOLLOWING CHAPTERS, we intend to help physician leaders plan their conversations with the target physician. Note that we use the word "plan" and not "script." All conversations, and coaching conversations, in particular, are personal and in-depth exchanges. As we often remind physician leaders engaging in these conversations, "The most important thing to say next is directly related to what the other person just said." It is not possible to script the other person's part in the meeting, so you'll need to be present, engaged, and prepared to pivot based on their reactions and responses. This doesn't mean you need to abandon your objectives or the key points you wish to emphasize in the conversation; it does mean you'll need to prepare differently than you would for grand rounds or a productivity report to your partners.

We are not suggesting that physician leaders become credentialed, professional coaches; however, we do recommend relying on the coaching competencies put forth by the International Coaching Federation (ICF), the most highly regarded accrediting and credentialing body for both training programs and coaches.[116]

Throughout the next two chapters, which focus on the process aspects of coaching conversations, we draw on ICF competencies such as cultivating trust and safety and evoking self-awareness while recognizing that you cannot adopt a pure coaching role given your responsibilities for the performance of the target physician and the team.

EARLY INTERVENTION

In Chapter 1, we emphasized the power of early intervention; however, the decision of exactly when to intervene is generally a bit cloudy. Physician leaders are likely to question whether an episode of disruptive behavior is an exception or aberration — the classic one-off from a physician's regular behavioral patterns. There is a natural tendency to avoid intervening under such uncertain circumstances.

Here, we will push just a bit. Our guidance is to judiciously intervene when you are first made aware of a disruptive episode. Our views are guided by two considerations.

First, by talking with the target physician, you may help them uncover and attune to what could be a blind spot in their interactions. In this regard, these interactions may increase the physician's self-awareness and help them become more sensitive to their behaviors and how they are being perceived by others.[29,106,117]

There is a second and more practical reason for this early response. Once you have been made aware of a disruptive event, it is likely not the first episode. Rather, events and actions have exceeded the threshold of intensity, and others now feel that their leader needs to be aware and involved.

There are some differences of opinion regarding the initial conversation (intervention) as well as subsequent meetings. Some experts feel that such meetings should not be one-on-one exchanges, arguing that the physician leader needs to have a third party present to corroborate and provide an objective assessment of what has been discussed and decided.[85] In this regard, the presence of a third party helps ameliorate a potential he-said, she-said outcome and is beneficial if legal action ensues.

Others suggest that an impartial physician should serve as the intermediary for the initial informal meeting. There is merit to this view. A physician colleague creates a less ominous presence than would one in a hierarchical position of formal leadership. A collegial encounter can signal concern and do so with a less formal and more helpful tone.

Still, others contend that one-on-one exchanges between the designated physician leader and target physician are preferable, as these exchanges provide greater confidentiality and reduce the number of individuals involved in interventional and remedial activities. Given these options — all quite credible — let's unpack the situation.

There is no definitive one-size-fits-all answer here. In general, we prefer to keep matters between the physician leader and target physician, thereby minimizing potential embarrassment, premature labeling of the physician as problematic, and stilted interactions among colleagues. Discretion is key; however, if you believe that the target physician is likely to become combative, likely to twist your ideas, or likely to insinuate the need for litigation, the presence of a third party may be beneficial. Typically, this is not the case. Yet, we must not be naïve. Special circumstances notwithstanding, we prefer dealing with issues at the local level between the physician leader and the target physician.

This initial step — your first intervention meeting — is best viewed as an informal conversation. We encourage you to meet in a comfortable setting. The casual setting is important, as it helps ameliorate the trappings of authority. While the meeting puts the target physician on alert, it also helps the physician leader learn of factors or underlying issues that may have contributed to or prompted the immediate episode. As such, leaders may discover areas where they are able to offer help and support.

Consider the following example, which, given the vagaries of life, is not uncommon. Susan, a seemingly well-adjusted physician, had some angry and dismissive interactions with her staff over the period of a week. When having a casual conversation with Susan, her physician leader started simply, "These situations have come to my attention. This doesn't seem like you. Is there anything going on?"

Given the opening, Susan shifted from her carefully guarded privacy and revealed that she was in the early, ugly phases of divorce. Of course, such awareness does not diminish the impact of Susan's behavior; however, the two were able to craft a plan of support, including some personal time to help Susan sort things through.

Even if such revelations are not forthcoming, this initial casual conversation is time well spent. For example, it establishes a base of support, which becomes even more critical if further interventions are needed. At the very least, target physicians know that their physician leaders are willing to listen, understand, support, and help. This sets an important conversational tone.

When a second episode occurs, the ante has been raised. Now, it is important to have a formal discussion. Here, the leader's concern is that the earlier episode was not a one-off. Further, the meeting signals to the target physician that their behaviors have not fallen from the leader's radar of concern. In this context, physician leaders should underline the need for disruptive behaviors to be checked, underscoring the unacceptable nature of those behaviors and specifying why such behaviors are problematic.

Of course, subsequent, repeated episodes require more deft handling, which we will turn to shortly. Here, leaders can reasonably share with the target physician that they are concerned that a pattern may be developing and, with that pattern, a rash of negative labels may be evolving. It is important to be direct in laying out the issues and concerns but also to focus on the transpersonal nature of the physician's work performance. While you are involved because you are the target physician's leader, they are ultimately searching for ways to feel effective, satisfied, and fulfilled as human beings.[117] Let's delve into this integrated and interactive process.

THE COMMUNICATION PROCESS:
THE FIRST MESSAGE

Physician leaders are analyzers, quick studies, and decision-makers. Accordingly, when meeting with a target physician, there is a tendency to get busy laying out the facts and stressing the need for change. We will get there; however, it's not the preferred starting point.

Two examples may help. For several years, we worked with a small group of 12 CEOs and presidents representing an array of organizations. Participants were selected to ensure that competing executives did not participate. The quarterly morning sessions were designed to be open and candid.

As we had hoped, once the group recognized and accepted our code of confidentiality, members helped one another with some complex and thorny issues; they were the kind of open discussions that top executives rarely have. One member of our group was Gene, CEO of a mid-sized manufacturing company. Gene looked and acted like a CEO, with gravitas and executive presence. He was also a savvy executive with keen analytic and financial skills.

Given these characteristics, it was unsettling to observe Gene as he entered the room for our regular session. Normally upbeat, his demeanor was clearly restrained. Gene asked to speak first as the session started because, as he told us, "I need help from this group."

Gene explained that due to some unexpected economic factors, not the least of which were labor issues that severely constricted demand from his primary corporate customer, he needed to downsize his business. He'd run all the numbers a hundred different ways. There was no option: staff reduction was needed, and it should be imminent.

Gene was open with the group. "I haven't slept in two days. This is the hardest decision I've ever had to make. When I took over, I worked my tail off to create a team culture, and now, I'll be letting part of our team go. I'm just sick about this."

One of his fellow CEOs asked Gene how he would handle the all-employee meeting that was only three days away. Gene replied, "I'm going to show them the data. Explain the economics of the situation. Help them see the analysis and recognize why these actions are needed for our future — really our survival. That's what I do, and it's what I must do here."

The voice of a relatively young behavioral scientist, a voice that sounded strikingly familiar, spoke up. "Gene, you certainly do have to provide them with the data and the analysis and the logic behind this move. But I'm not sure that's where you start." Gene bristled a bit, "What do you mean?"

I stepped into the danger zone. "Gene, I think you should lead with your heart. Tell them what you just told us. Don't belabor it, but be authentic. Tell them that you've had sleepless nights, that this is your team — your work family, that it's the hardest decision you've ever had to make. Do that first. Then move to the facts."

With no desire for overstatement, at our next meeting, Gene shared that the emotional opening built immediate rapport and enhanced the team's receptivity to an unpleasant message. It also sparked a creative discussion of ways to trim expenses — ideas that were helpful and well-received.

We saw it played out a few years later as we worked with Ed, a distinguished surgeon and service line physician leader. Ed was struggling to deal with Josh, a surgeon who displayed far too many disruptive behaviors in far too many circumstances. Here's how Ed started the communication: "Josh. You remind me of me about 20 years ago. You have excellent surgical skills, and you care deeply about your patients and their families. You are an asset to our department and contribute to the strong surgical outcomes we boast."

As a leader, Ed would get to the point in a few minutes, talk about Josh's disruptive behaviors, explain what was at stake, and push (with no equivocation) for change. But first, Ed led with his heart, showing Josh that he was valued, that he was significant, and that he was needed. Such an approach may not change everything, but it can make a difference.

Let's think this through just a bit. When you meet with your target physician, they recognize the agenda, expecting the hammer of condemnation to fall and to fall with force. They can be defensive and poised for a fight.[118] Instead, you offer an expression of their value. You are not minimizing their disruptive actions, and you are not dismissing their unacceptable impact. Rather, you are approaching them as valued colleagues. Defensiveness may not be eliminated or even blunted very much, but the tone and perspective have shifted.

Why don't leaders typically use this starting point? Many see it as a sign of weakness, a chink in one's leadership armor that will surely be exploited by a troubled and problematic colleague. Some may argue that in the fast-paced world of modern healthcare, we do not have time for the "soft," collegial opening. Here, one may argue that the physician leader needs to get to the point and do so quickly. We counter this by reminding you that this is only your opening, not the entirety of your message. The meeting and conversation have just begun.

Two of the fundamental ICF competencies at play here are the coaching mindset and cultivating trust and safety. While "maintaining a mindset that is open, curious, flexible and client-centered," an effective coach "demonstrates respect for the client's identity, perceptions, style and language" and "acknowledges and respects the client's unique talents and insights."[116] Providing a person-oriented, developmentally focused tone is very much the point.

Further, evidence suggests that the opening — the first 30 to 60 seconds of your interaction with a target physician — sets the tone for subsequent conversations and actions.[96] As Stephen Trezeciak and Anthony Mazzerelli note, a positive perspective can be set between parties in as little as 30 seconds.[119] Accordingly, we encourage you to use a three-step introduction to the conversation: *connect,* establish the *noble cause,* and project an *other-focused intent.*

First, *connect* with your target physician by beginning with statements of affirmation and significance. For example, "Dave, you are an important part of our team. You have strong clinical skills. I want you to thrive as a physician and as part of our team."

Second, establish the *noble cause* and help the physician see how they are part of the broader picture. "Dave, our work in our specialty area is gaining traction; we have new opportunities, such as the new residency program. We see you as a vital part of realizing them."

Third is a simple statement of *other-focused intent.* For example, "Dave, you have strong potential, as well as opportunities for growth and further development. I want you to thrive as a physician and as part of our team. That's why I need to take time to meet with you."

These three simple points may not seem like much; however, they set a tone that is positive and growth-oriented rather than punitive, which is likely what the target physician is expecting. Again, this introduction does not need to take more than a minute. Make eye contact, smile, deliver the points with a warmth that signals sincerity and authenticity, and don't rush — all important steps to create the mood for what follows.

Before progressing to the next stage — that of delivering the *primary message of expectation for change* — leave room for the target physician's response. It is likely that the target physician may state that they are not quite sure why the meeting with you is taking place. That can be your opening to progress. If this does not evolve naturally, it is your responsibility to forward the action. "Dave, let me delve into the reason we are meeting."

FOCUS AND LIMIT THE AGENDA

Physician leaders and target physicians are both quite busy. As such, once leaders find time to sit down for a conversation, there is a temptation to use the meeting to lay out every issue and concern that has been brewing for months (or longer). While pragmatically understandable, this is a mistake. Instead, we encourage leaders to *pinpoint and focus,* zeroing in on one or two critical themes that we must do right now to advance the process of progress.[112,120]

There are at least two reasons for such a selective focus. First, leaders draw attention to the most significant concerns without risking a breakdown in clarity that comes with a broader and more inclusive approach. Second, it keeps the target physician from being overwhelmed.

The idea of limiting the agenda also draws on the well-researched themes of goal-setting theory. Here, leaders are better served emphasizing tangible actions that are clear, specific, challenging, and direct rather than simply encouraging the target physician to "do their best."[121]

A BLUEPRINT FOR THE NEXT STEP: COACHING

As noted above, we do not recommend scripting your conversation, but we do recommend preparing for it by identifying key points and expectations, acknowledging the areas in which you'd like to create or amplify awareness, and preparing to balance how much information you put into the interaction with how much energy you'll draw out.

Herminia Ibarra and Anne Scoular suggest that leaders master the "energy out" piece of this equation first: listening, supporting, and drawing insights out of the target physician that helps them resolve the concerns on their own.[122] Once the target physician feels heard and supported, there is room for more direction — advice, solutions, and performance expectations with consequences, which is the focus of the next chapter. Accordingly, this first meeting is about mobilizing the target physician to make a change.

A helpful model for drawing energy out of the target physician is the use of the GROW (Goal, Reality, Options, Will) model, most often attributed to John Whitmore in his book *Coaching for Performance*,[123] although he admits that the chronology of the approach crystallized much earlier than the terms.[117] We outline the model here and provide an example of how one might approach Susan (an earlier target physician) if her angry and dismissive reactions continued after our initial conversation and ostensible solution described at the outset of this chapter.

The first step in our plan should be to identify the *goal*. What needs to be different as a result of this conversation and the developmental work that follows? Of course, *you* have a goal in this situation, perhaps several: fewer complaints, more team harmony, and the long-term and often more subjective impact on productivity and patient experience. And the department, practice, hospital, and healthcare system have goals they need to reach as well.

But first, we want to surface *Susan's* goal. Going in with the assumption that she doesn't want to be perceived as angry or dismissive, we can ask what it is that she does want. Does she want more efficiency and fewer disruptions during her workday? Does she want to improve her ability to set emotional boundaries between what is going on outside of work and how she shows up with her staff? Does she want to avoid uncomfortable conversations with you at all costs?

Once you've surfaced Susan's goals, you can help her see the connection between the larger goals, which confirms your authority in evoking the conversation and reminds her that she is part of a larger effort.

The second step is to clarify the *reality*. What do we know about Susan's performance in relation to the goals — hers and those of the physician leader and the organization? You may start with the complaints you've heard or the changes in Susan's demeanor you've witnessed. If efficiency and fewer disruptions come up, you can suggest that efficiency is something you'd like to see too and explore the specific inefficiencies present. It is likely that Susan is not experiencing greater inefficiency but simply greater sensitivity to inefficiency that has always been present.

Before moving on, we need to know where the "You are here" arrow is on the board. We cannot generate ideas about how to move forward without knowing where we are.

The next step is to generate *options*. Your main role here may be to help Susan get unstuck. She may believe there is nothing she can do until the stress of her divorce has subsided. If that's the case, you may ask her to imagine that the stress of the divorce has already subsided, and then ask what would be the first thing she would do.

In most cases, people like Susan might say, "I would take a break and reset my relationships with my staff." Perhaps there is some small part she can do now — talking with staff about what she is facing and asking for grace and patience.

Or, she may say, "When this is over, I'm going to enjoy coming in for early procedures again. Joy in my work is just so hard to access on zero sleep." Perhaps an option now is to adjust clinical hours, trading time in the procedure room with someone who has the flexibility to take patients in the early morning hours.

You may also know of some resources that could be helpful, such as a stress-reduction retreat the hospital system is supporting or access to a scribe on a temporary basis that may reduce Susan's workload and recapture some efficiency.

At this point, our only requirement is that options are directionally appropriate. With each option, run a validity check: will taking this approach move us closer from where we are to the goal we have set? Ultimately, as you move to the next step (*will*), you may break options down into micro goals, embarrassingly simple actions that move your target physician forward. If the option of shifting her procedures to later in the day is appealing, a micro goal may be to determine her ideal schedule, say 10:00 am –1:00 pm rather than 7:00 am –10:00 am. Or, it may be to make a list of her room requirements that you can forward to your dyad partner to see if an alternate space is available for later appointments.

The last piece of the GROW model is *will*. What will Susan commit to doing? At this point, you may ask that she try to change a few small things and state that you will follow up with her in one to two weeks max. In subsequent conversations, you may need to provide more formal expectations and performance requirements. This is the focus of the next chapter as we move more deliberately to action and accountability.

ADDITIONAL CONSIDERATIONS FOR A FORMAL CONVERSATION

So far, we have discussed a recommended outline of the first formal conversation:

1. The First Message
   a. Connection
   b. Noble cause
   c. Other-focused intent
2. Focused Agenda

3. Drawing Energy Out
   a. Goals
   b. Reality
   c. Options
   d. Will

In this section, we will explore three special areas of consideration: pace, tone, and understanding. Each area will be important for physician leaders who are engaging target physicians in developmental conversations — the first formal conversation as well as subsequent touch points, both formal and informal.

While these considerations and suggestions may seem basic, they should not be overlooked. Further, we hope that leaders can ingrain these ideas into their conversational style, as attention to them enhances most communication exchanges.

Pace

Physician leaders should consciously *pace down,* slowing the rate of speech and using brief moments of silence to moderate the flow of communication. Pacing down runs counter to the defensive energy that emanates from the target physicians. As emotions rise, there is a marked tendency to increase the rate of speech. The tendency becomes consuming, leading all parties to ramp up the pace of discussion.

Slowing the pace allows the target physician to better receive and grasp the messages being delivered. In short, they have a better chance of getting their arms around the issues and needs, as well as the impact of their actions.

Further, slowing the pace allows for a more reflective discussion. It allows the other party to interpret and internalize the points being shared. It breeds better listening and encourages a two-way conversation. Slowing the pace also signals to your target physician that the current conversation is important and worthy of taking some time.

One way to slow the pace is to query the target physician at regular intervals to ensure their understanding. This should be a straightforward question. Simply asking, "Does this make sense?" after each key point may be enough if the target party is open and willing to provide honest impressions regarding the clarity of points. Another useful question is to ask the target party, "What are you hearing?" or "What does this last point mean for you?" What we think is direct and clear may be filtered by the other party in such a way that the interpretation and meaning are skewed and not fully reflective of the message we intended to deliver.

Tone

As the leader, you set the tone for the conversation that will take place. Don't allow your supportive and remediative tone to be minimized or thrown off course by bothersome or dismissive mannerisms that the target physician may employ. Here, we suggest three responses: (1) affirmation, (2) help and support, and (3) core values and codes of conduct.

First, you've likely started the conversation by *affirming the value and significance* of the target physician to the clinical goals of your unit. You may need to revisit this several times during the conversation. As we have already discussed, physicians who display chronic disruptive behaviors typically have strong technical skills and provide high-quality patient care. Reinforce these contributions; underscore the physician's talents and significance.

These statements are not attempts at ingratiation. Rather, they should be open and authentic expressions of the physician's value. The hope here is that such an approach establishes positive affect, which is especially important when the target physician is likely to be defensive, angry, and expecting to be chastised.[118]

Second, reiterate to the target physician that your goal is to be *helpful and supportive* rather than simply being critical. Leaders should strive to help target physicians understand the leader's motives. Hopefully, these include a sincere concern for helping the physician. Leaders should help target physicians recognize that the leader is dedicated to the target's development and growth — themes that will foster interpersonal rapport and enhance the broader goals of your unit.

Here, we encourage physician leaders to take a direct and open approach, an approach best achieved with genuine and expansive questioning.[124] For example, the physician leader may pose an exploratory question to the target physician: "How can I help?" "What do you need from me to help with the situation we have just discussed?"

Indeed, it is possible (perhaps even likely) that the target physician may deflect blame toward others or suggest actions that the leader is unable or unwilling to pursue. However, the questions and responses are valuable. The target physician learns that the leader is willing to help. The target physician recognizes that the leader desires to consider the target physician's perspectives. Additionally, the questions offer a direct look into the mindset and views that frame the target physician's actions. All of these are valuable pieces for making progress.

Third, outlining the *core values and any codes of conduct* that exist for your unit and organization is a way to depersonalize your requests for collegiality in addressing the issue at hand. In most cases, these are readily available — perhaps even included within the practice's mission statement.

For example, one organization with whom we have worked openly lists core values and behavioral expectations, including such themes as personal worth and dignity for all people, collaboration and teamwork, the emotional well-being of all employees, and a supportive work environment. Including such value themes underscores the relevance and importance of the conversation and why it is taking place. These pieces also establish concerns about actions that deviate from accepted values and norms of conduct.

Understanding

In his book *Supercommunicators,* Charles Duhigg emphasizes that communication is a learning conversation where we try to understand one another.[125] It may be tempting to overlook this step, especially given the disturbance the target physician seems to be creating. Yet, everyone has a story, and everyone has a personal perspective. Further, as noted earlier, seeking understanding does not dismiss questionable behavior, and it certainly does not diminish the need for change. Rather, it approaches the other party as an individual who probably views events through a different lens.

As analytical thinkers, physician leaders typically prepare for any physician meeting by digging into the evidence and reviewing any complaints. However, leaders must fight the urge to enter the initial conversation, convinced that they have all the information needed to understand what is taking place and what actions need to occur.

The target physician has a unique perspective, and it may differ markedly from other views that the leader has ascertained. Indeed, another ICF core competency is *listening*, "focusing on what the client is and is not saying to fully understand what is being communicated."[116]

Moreover, if leaders listen and are open and receptive, the target physician is likely to share new data. While this data may be self-serving, protective, and skewed, it should be heard and considered. At the least, leaders gain a broader and richer sense of the events and factors that surround disruptive behaviors. Again, physician leaders build a relationship and sense of partnership, which can be critical.

CIRCLING BACK TO EXPECTATIONS AND NEEDS

At this point, you have connected with the target physician, discussed expectations for change, engaged the physician in his or her own development, and listened and responded to the feedback and perspectives that they have provided. You have also considered pace, tone, and understanding.

Before leaving this initial meeting, carefully and concisely define your behavioral expectations once more. Vague and poorly defined phrases such as "do better" or "make some changes" are insufficient and unlikely to yield meaningful change. As noted earlier, there is considerable evidence that "do your best" goals have limited behavioral impact.[121] Clarify your expectations and needs, present them in tangible and pragmatic behavioral terms, and set a short timeframe for observing directionally appropriate change and following up.

At this juncture, reiterating *why* these behavioral expectations are important is essential. If all this seems a bit redundant, it is necessary to repeat it at the close of this first formal meeting. The target physician may need time to process and "get their arms around" the messages you are presenting, but they should leave with clarity on what you expect.

Check for understanding. What you say and what you intend may not be what others have received and heard. Interpretations often vary, driven by each person's needs, as well as a logical bias to refrain from admitting a need for change. As such, the powers of selective perception are pervasive, helping protect both ego and established habits.

It's useful to keep in mind the emotional impact that your target physician is likely experiencing. Research indicates that physicians generally have a high need for achievement and a high need to avoid failure, and we would expect physicians who display disruptive behaviors to have similar motivations. Consequently, they are likely to interpret your messages as signals of their failure — an awareness that's hard to accept, even among the most emotionally aware of us.

You may need to be quite basic here, asking your target physician, "What are you hearing?" Repeat your expectations and reiterate why these expectations are critical. This is a process that demands both patience and resolve, listening and responding, but moving forward.

In the next chapter, we discuss the follow-up meetings. In some cases, they become more directive and consequential. In other cases, follow-up conversations are more supportive for the purpose of inspiring continued development.

SUMMARY CHECKLIST

This chapter has been largely a checklist. However, for convenience, let's look at a few key items:

- After a casual conversation, a more formal conversation is required, but one that is aimed at mobilizing the target physician rather than solving the problem.
- While physician leaders are not expected to become professional coaches, they should still adopt a coaching mindset to effectively guide target physicians.
- Plan conversations rather than scripting them, as coaching requires adapting to the dynamic flow of dialogue.
- Be present and attentive, ready to pivot based on the responses of the other person.
- Maintain objectives and key points, attend to pace and tone, and ensure understanding.

CHAPTER 7

Moving to Action

···

FOLLOWING THE FRAMEWORKS presented in Chapter 6, physician leaders have built the foundation for behavior change. They have identified the gap between expressed behaviors and those deemed appropriate and acceptable for the unit, and they have invited the target physician to be an active participant in immediate behavior change and lasting interpersonal development.

With a lighter touch to start, leaders communicated so that target physicians could grasp the impact — the negative ramifications — of the target behaviors under consideration. At this point, leaders made it clear that change must take place and that the current behavioral paths the target physician has chosen are unacceptable.

In some cases, the target physician engages earnestly, and follow-up meetings deepen the learning from changing behavior and committing to additional action. The physician leader becomes a trusted partner in leadership development, encouraging positive change and monitoring the health of the relationships with team members, which may result in further coaching and development.

In other cases, change is not forthcoming, so physician leaders may need to be more direct, firmly communicating that the *status quo* is untenable and the gap must be closed.[126] The target physician must move from engaging in developmental conversations (talk) to directed behavioral changes (new actions). A detailed plan of action is necessary, and the unsuccessful execution or implementation of that plan must come with material consequences. In this chapter, we deal with the challenge of setting meaningful performance goals when there does not seem to be an instinctive, collaborative reaction to the initial conversation.

While you may be prepared to read about how to shift gears here, moving to a dictatorial approach, we appeal to your identity as a progressive leader and developmental coach, starting with a caveat. While it may be tempting to take an authoritative stance, instructing or telling target physicians how they must behave, we encourage a more direct but similarly interactive strategy. The plan of action should be jointly determined by you and your target physician for at least three reasons.

First, when target physicians are directly involved in developing the plan, they have a deeper sense of commitment to ensuring the plan succeeds. Not surprisingly, research reveals that when people are involved in setting goals and plans, their acceptance is enhanced.[127]

Second, it is important that target physicians take responsibility and accountability for their actions.[96] Research shows that people who set their own goals show more commitment to achieving the goals, although they may need accountability from their leader to ensure that the goal is sufficient.[128] The plan of action must evolve from an open discussion of approaches and the desired impact.

Third, physicians, like other highly educated professionals, often balk at being told what they should do. As we noted previously, overly directive behavior runs counter to the fundamental needs and motives of physicians.

Of course, this push for personal accountability can be tricky, as the target physician may face conflicting realities — they are being asked to commit to changes that they may not feel are necessary in the first place. Ideally, we want the target physician to be an active participant, a partner in constructing a plan of action that leads to greater personal effectiveness and a more positive impact on the team. In this manner, target physician growth and development are enhanced.

However, the second reality is persistent and unequivocal. Even if the target physician doesn't see the need for substantial behavior change, change must take place; doing nothing or moving in non-relevant directions cannot be tolerated. Here, it may be necessary to drive home your expectations by clarifying the problematic behavior that has brought the target physician to this point.

THE EVIDENCE

As logical and methodical practitioners, physician leaders can be expected to have gathered the evidence and the facts of the situation well before the initial conversation; however, when it comes to communicating them to the target physician, the task is trickier than it may seem. For example, Kerry Patterson and colleagues emphasize that we all have different views of the facts.[92] While technically inexact — a fact, by definition, connotes truth or objective reality — the point still resonates. Behavioral issues are always open for interpretation, and perceptions of facts may differ widely. Recall that physicians displaying chronic disruptive behaviors often have skewed views of their own behaviors and how those behaviors affect others.

Often, clear, objective data are not readily available. Here, it is important to offer specific behavioral examples. As noted in Chapter 3, consider the constellation of factors: those interrelated realities that may reasonably affect the behavior in question. Of course, finding evidence can take many forms, all driven by the search for a logical, fair, and unbiased view of the situation and its impact. Searching for evidence should be a fact-revealing exercise, not one guided by a priori assumptions and beliefs. This is another reason why being cognizant of your personal emotions toward the situation and toward the target physician is critical. In this regard, Matt Mazurek advises that when we receive a complaint, we should be curious but not judgmental.[85]

We recommend carefully defining the disruptive behavior that is of concern at the outset of this follow-up conversation and clearly detailing why these target behaviors are unacceptable. Here, we suggest a four-step process: (1) define the behavior clearly and specifically; (2) clearly define expectations — the behaviors that should and must occur; (3) explain why the desired behavior(s) are so important; and (4) circle back to check with the target physician for understanding.

You will notice that some of these steps were also part of the initial conversation, but here, we are more directive in our approach. As Herminia Ibarra and Anne Scoular[122] suggest, we are focusing more heavily on "information in" after we've done all we can to "pull energy out."

Clearly defining the target disruptive behavior first helps remove ambiguity. By starting here, the target physician is also able to mentally focus on the behavioral issues at hand. Clarity and specificity are key. An example may help. Imploring physicians to always conduct themselves in a "professional manner" is an important statement. However, it is also too open-ended, too loosely defined, and likely to be subjected to idiosyncratic interpretations. As such, the admonition to behave in a professional manner is unlikely to provide needed guidance and necessary guardrails.[129]

By next emphasizing expected behaviors, the gap between expressed and desired behaviors should become clear. Take your time here. Be sure the target physician is aware of the gap. Continue to focus on behaviors. While subtle, focusing on behavior and gaps in behavior reinforces that remediating disruptive behavior is our goal, rather than chastising the person – our target physician.

In this regard, the Tennessee Medical Foundation argues that we must help the target physician see that the behavior in question deviates (and deviates strongly) from the norms of the peer group.[24] As such, it is incumbent on the physician leader to clearly express the behaviors that *are* acceptable and expected. In this regard, we want the target physician to recognize that a *gap* exists between expected/normative behavior and what they are expressing.[96]

The next step is often omitted, and again, that is a mistake. Take the time to explain (or reiterate) *why* the expectations and desired behaviors are so important, a critical theme that has been the focus of groundbreaking work by Simon Sinek.[130] The *why* is neither redundant nor obvious.

Recall that target physicians often lack insight regarding how their behavior affects others.[81] Link the *why* back to your statements of vision, core values, and the noble cause when appropriate. Discuss the impact on staff morale and overall culture. Explain how stress levels are being accelerated by the disruptive behavior. You may even explain that when staff feels diminished, they become tenuous and less likely to share information, all of which may affect patient well-being.

The impacts we discussed in Chapter 1 should offer some thoughts to consider as you frame and deliver the *why* message. Consistent with current theory on behavioral change, it is fundamental that target physicians realize that change must take place since the *status quo* is unacceptable.[126]

Now comes a more nuanced step: provide the target physician with *legitimate voice,* the opportunity to talk and express themselves. Slow down. Listen. This may be a rambling oration laden with excuses, diversions, and heightened emotion. Check for clarity. Summarize what the person is saying. The target physician must feel that they have been heard and understood. By listening, asking questions, and seeking to understand the other's views, you are neither accepting nor legitimizing their behaviors.

At some point, it will be necessary to return to the topic of desired behaviors and, once again, briefly note why such behavior is so important. Redundancy here is appropriate and needed. Remember, the target physician is probably in a defensive mode at this point. Accordingly, they need to hear the message more than once, and it is wise to follow up with an email to document what you have concluded.

It is not unusual that the target physician may deny engaging in the behaviors you have described. On one hand, they may truly be unaware of their actions and especially the impact others are experiencing. On the other hand, there is a good chance that they are dismissing or minimizing their behaviors. Our experience suggests that the latter case is far more common than the first.

We encourage two approaches. First, come to the meeting with as much evidence and hard data as you can gather. Hard data — explosive emails, missed deadlines, and any matter that is documented — is much more difficult to dismiss. However, we recognize that such data is often limited or non-existent. So, we move to a second approach: sharing perceptions and impressions. For example, it can be useful to note that "You are being perceived as overly aggressive" or, better yet, outlining your own experiences with the physician's disruptive behavior.

THE ACTION-PLANNING PROCESS

When target physicians are apprised of the gap between what they are currently doing and what is required, they confront a dynamic cognitive process.[131] Initially, they must agree that a gap exists. Once a shared understanding of the action-impact gap is in place, target physicians must recognize the debilitating impact of the gap. Finally, they must accept responsibility for closing the gap, planning and executing different behavioral actions that are more likely to achieve the desired impact. Each step in this cognitive process is likely steeped in pushback.

At this point, your expectations of the target physician should be quite clear, and it is time to ask *them* to generate objectives, action steps, and success metrics. Here, the physician leader behaves as a gatekeeper, listening and delivering candid feedback regarding overall objectives, action steps, or success metrics.

At times, target physicians may suggest plans that are simply insufficient. Some proposed plans may skirt the issues, failing to address the central issues of behavioral change. In such cases, leaders must be clear and straightforward. For example, "Glen, I hear what you are suggesting. However, I don't see how changing your OR schedule to work with a different team ameliorates the counter-productive emotional outbursts we need to address." And then, the ball is returned to their court.

It's perfectly fine to suggest ideas, behaviors, and approaches — these become especially important when target physicians seem to be struggling to find reasonable answers. Suggest — don't impose. However, do not retreat from the corrective actions and new behaviors that must be attained. This is indeed a gentle dance: prod, listen, respond, and ask for more.

Recall that some target physicians are masters at creating excuses — excuses that discount or minimize their disruptive actions. In addition, they are adept at deflecting blame. One key responsibility for physician leaders is to inject a dose of reality. Your goal here is to remain focused on the target physicians and their behavior. When presented with an array of distractions and obfuscations, your best leadership approach is to return to the presence of the gap and the recognition that the gap must be closed.

Further, you should not allow the focus to shift to others (nurses, staff, physician colleagues, upper administration) despite the target physician's pleas that much of the fault is with others. Be direct, encouraging the target physician to address what they must and can do rather than cloud the matter with excuses and deflections.

Strive to be clear and decisive without being strident or confrontational. Avoid arguing — it's a dangerous trek to attempt to address each excuse that's offered — an excursion that takes you off the desired path. Again, you are reaching for a plan of action that places accountability on what the target physician can affect, not the tangent of concerns that they cannot, which subsequently lets them off the hook for taking action at all.

A STRUCTURED APPROACH

The plan of action should address at least five interrelated items. First, the immediate goal is stated. Second, the action steps (behaviors) that will be enacted to meet the goal are delineated. Third, target dates for action completion are included. Fourth, the means of evaluating progress (or lack of progress) should be noted. Fifth and finally are the adjustments that follow the evaluation. We hope this will be a living document that the target physician can use to guide and modify their remediative behaviors.

Without belaboring the matter, SMART goals — specific, measurable, achievable, relevant, and time-bound — are preferred.[132] All dimensions of SMART goals are important. However, for our target physicians, specificity and time (time-sensitive) are especially critical because you'll want the goals to mirror behavioral expectations (which are specific), and there is some urgency to change behavior if we are engaged in this conversation in the first place.

While a great deal of research supports the SMART goal components, it is important to note that goals may narrow the target physician's focus.[128] This may be intended and necessary, but we encourage the physician leader to ensure expectations are set that cover all key performance metrics. For instance, a leader who is focused on building relationships with her team may not have time to complete charts or attend staff meetings. Make clear what expectations may not suffer as a result of the focus on the target physician's development.

Once complete, review the plan of action. Be sure you are comfortable with the action steps involved. Pose some tough questions. Do these steps further the goal, or are they easy, low-hanging fruit steps that fail to address the central points needed for goal attainment?

We always ask those whom we are coaching a couple of tough questions here. You may wish to follow the pattern with your target physicians. For example, "Explain to me exactly how the proposed action steps will reach your expressed goal and help close the gap in expectations." Don't shy away from the follow-on question, "Can you see yourself actually doing the actions you have outlined?" At this point, if you have concerns about any of the proposed actions or the target physician's sense of commitment, say so. Further reflection and discussion are needed.

Let's reconsider an important point. There is a difference between being firm, decisive, and focused and being overly demanding and directive. Much of this has to do with the tone of development and support that you have previously established, but take care not to diminish the headway you've made during previous steps in the process. Given all this, let's consider a recent encounter.

Jocelyn is a new physician leader who inherited Michael as part of her team. Jocelyn realized that concerns about Michael were well-known within the unit (and beyond). However, she also recognized that the unit's previous leader had taken the path of tolerance toward Michael, dismissing or diminishing the impact of his disruptive behaviors — after all, Michael was a good doctor with positive patient feedback and outcomes.

Jocelyn now faced a new challenge. Michael had once again lashed out at Mari, a physician colleague. Apparently, Michael was upset with Mari for requesting a consultation regarding a patient — a consultation that added a new variable to an already packed day. Unfortunately, Michael's tirade was carried out in front of four staff members, adding considerably to the frustration and resentment Mari felt. She brought the issue to Jocelyn.

After some initial conversations with Jocelyn, Michael agreed that he must take constructive action regarding Mari. He set a goal of "working to have a better relationship with Mari." Wisely, Jocelyn recognized that this goal, as presented, was far too vague and open-ended. It lacked behavioral clarity and specificity. As she pushed Michael a bit, he relented, "OK, my goal will be to meet with Mari." Better, perhaps, but still not quite on the mark. Jocelyn decided that it would be prudent to accept this statement and turn to address specific actions.

"Okay, Michael. A meeting sounds good. When will it take place?" Michael hedged. "Well, we are all busy. I'll try to get with her over the next few weeks." Here, Jocelyn asserted herself. "Michael, we need more than that. The issues are critical. The meeting needs to take place soon, by the end of the week. The more time that goes by, the more gossip takes place, and the damage simply expands."

Michael shot back, saying that the gossip was not his fault, but Jocelyn recognized the deflection and recentered her expectations. "This week, Michael. Can you do that?" With a bit of thought, Michael noted that both he and Mari had administrative time on Thursday afternoon, and he would schedule a meeting with Mari then.

A small victory, perhaps. Jocelyn played on her momentum. "How long will you set for the meeting?" Both agreed that at least 30 minutes should be blocked. As a good leader and coach, Jocelyn probed further. "Michael, what will you do or say when you have the meeting this Thursday?" Having worked with Jocelyn previously as a participant in our workshop series for physician leaders, we were pleased that she suggested that Michael consider our three-part model: (1) apologize, (2) listen, and (3) commit to a new set of behaviors.

Michael agreed that an apology was a reasonable starting point, so Jocelyn moved into action, helping Michael frame a message of apology that demonstrated he was taking responsibility for his actions. They discussed the remaining steps, and Michael agreed that he had a plan for meeting with Mari. Jocelyn moved ahead, "This sounds like a solid plan, Michael. Let's connect on Friday. I want to hear how the meeting with Mari went."

Jocelyn's decision to meet with Michael after his Thursday meeting to help close the loop was important — a key piece of ongoing developmental coaching. In addition, she is becoming part of the process of evaluating the efficacy of the actions Michael has taken. Here, we encourage leader coaches to move beyond broad questions. While asking, "How did the meeting with Mari go?" is a good starting point, it falls short of its developmental potential.

Three key pieces frame the follow-up meeting with Michael, and they are related to yet another ICF competency: facilitating growth by "integrating new awareness, insight or learning into their worldview and behaviors."[116] First, Jocelyn asked how Mari responded to the meeting and to Michael's apology. Second, she pressed Michael to identify "what seemed to work, what actions or behaviors seemed to resonate with Mari, and enhanced efforts to repair the relationship." The third point fosters further development: "Michael, what would you do differently if you had a chance to make some changes — a sort of reboot of the meeting?"

In this three-step process, Jocelyn is helping Michael monitor his behavior more consciously. She is also encouraging him to make regular behavioral alterations, hopefully building stronger and deeper understanding not only with Mari but in his overall interpersonal interactions. We recommend these three steps as a follow-up to virtually any action item on the target physician's plan: what was the response, what worked, and what did you learn that can be helpful going forward?

CONSEQUENCES AND RAMIFICATIONS

Experts agree that an important component in the process of addressing disruptive behaviors is to outline clear consequences or ramifications for noncompliance, articulating what happens if disruptive behaviors persist.[133,134] The issue of ramifications is tricky and demands careful consideration.

Often, we consider ramifications from a purely punitive perspective. One complication here is that the leader must be willing to actually deliver the ramifications once they have been expressed to the target physician. Indeed, failure to do so undermines a leader's credibility.

It can be useful to frame ramifications not as punishments you deliver but as consequences of noncompliance in terms of the target physician's values or reputation. In other words, frame ramifications in terms of what is important to or desired by the target physician, clearly noting how those desires will be harmed or thwarted if the target disruptive behaviors are not ameliorated. Here, we are structuring ramifications to create motivational potential for our target.[135]

Let's continue our example of Jocelyn and Michael. As already noted, Jocelyn knew that although previous leaders had had some limited conversations with Michael, no meaningful or lasting change in his behavior had occurred.

In assessing the situation, Jocelyn felt that previous remediations "lacked teeth," failing to affect Michael in terms that he cared about. She did a little digging and found that Michael wanted to assume a leadership role, particularly in a proposed expansion to the service line. She recognized that this leadership aspiration was important to Michael and part of his personal plan for the future. Accordingly, Jocelyn approached ramifications, considering this knowledge as a point of leverage.

She was direct and clear. "Michael, another disruptive episode like the one with Mari will require that I file a formal report with Human Resources. That report will be part of your record. As we both know, such a report will be considered by executive leadership when judging your capacity for any future leadership role." People are motivated to change when their self-interests are brought into the equation. Importantly, Jocelyn had not delivered an idle threat. Michael understood what was at play and knew that Jocelyn would address further indiscretions just as she had outlined.

At times, physician leaders may have to impose consequences that the target physician is not enamored with. For example, the Tennessee Medical Foundation lists six areas of training that may be beneficial for target physicians. These include anger management, conflict resolution, sensitivity training, communication skills, impulse control training, and basic processes of behavioral modification.[24]

Accordingly, you may find it beneficial to insist that target physicians participate in internal (if available) or external workshops to hone these skill areas. At times, it may even be beneficial to provide short-term executive coaching where an outside coach specializing in physician matters helps the target physician better address needed changes and how they can be achieved.

A caveat here is important: The use of external coaches should not substitute for the physician leader continuing to monitor, help, and support the target physician in an ongoing developmental manner. The worst course of action occurs when the presence of an external coach leads overworked physician leaders to assume that matters are in someone else's capable hands.

Of course, continued failure at remediation will require more extensive and more extreme measures, depending on the prevalence and intensity of the disruptive behaviors. Such actions may include (but are not limited to) getting another leader, such as the chief medical officer involved, the involvement of your internal medical board or committee that addresses such matters, partial loss or suspension of privileges, and ultimately denying reappointment.[24]

A final point must be noted: For most leaders, it's a challenge to carry through and impose the ramifications that have been established because although you are the physician leader, the target physician is a professional colleague and sometimes a friend. Recognize that your credibility is being tested. Judiciously following the plan of action, replete with consequences, is part of your leadership role. While it is not easy, it is essential to retain overall team progress, a sense of reasonable equity, and a culture of trust.

A WINDING PATH OF GROWTH AND DEVELOPMENT

Let's continue with Michael's story. Jocelyn made the decision to "stay close" to Michael, checking in with him on a regular basis. Given the tendency of difficult people to backslide, this approach is both laudatory and necessary. It also runs counter to a common instinct of minimizing potentially difficult encounters.

Let us be clear: stay close, communicate regularly, and keep those check-ins coming. Contrary to a common concern, these contacts are not a form of micro-management. Instead, they are prudent moves taken in the presence of persistent disruptive behavior. Keep in mind that this relatively constant flow of communication would be unnecessary if troublesome behavior were not present.

In our example, Michael got serious and made considerable progress. Jocelyn provided reinforcement and encouragement for the progress made. His path of improvement was not a linear pattern of growth; he did not suddenly become an enlightened new being. Yet, Michael was diligent and respectful for quite a while. Others noticed his efforts as he strived for intentional change.

Two months in, under considerable stress with troubling patient outcomes, Michael had another explosion. However, his response to the nurse who had incurred his wrath took a strikingly different posture. With enhanced self-awareness, Michael delivered a sincere apology, which the nurse accepted.

Now, Jocelyn faced a quandary — a decision that was as much about "feel" as it was about "process" and "credibility." Of course, she met with Michael, which was consistent with her regular check-ins. After talking with Michael, Jocelyn decided to extend some leniency — a decision driven by Michael's progress, timely apology, and the nurse's acceptance. However, she again explained the consequences of further episodes. Importantly, Michael expressed understanding and underscored his intention to continue his progress.

There is no hard and fast rule here. Jocelyn weighed the issues and made an informed decision. We were impressed by Jocelyn's sensitivity. We were even more impressed by her recognition that Michael needed support as he diligently worked through a process of change, recognizing that habitual dynamics are hard to overcome.

You may disagree with her decision; however, this is the process of interpersonal finesse that all successful leaders must navigate. In our minds, Jocelyn was not dodging her responsibility; rather, she was considering the entire context of how hard it is to enact behavioral change. Further, she sensed that Michael was sincere, as she had seen evidence of his efforts and his progress. Keep in mind that we are dealing with dynamic and idiosyncratic people — talented and proud. Simplistic and programmable formulas fail to capture the interrelated dynamics that are taking place.

We would love to tell you that, given Jocelyn's thoughtful and principled attention, the situation with Michael was resolved, and everyone lived happily ever after. That story would be cleaner and easier to deliver. Unfortunately, only 10 days later, Michael had another explosive and disruptive episode that forced Jocelyn's hand.

Here, she turned to the HR ramifications, as she had previously promised. Michael was distraught and, within a relatively short time, left the practice. Jocelyn's colleagues lauded her for courageously addressing what everyone knew was a problematic situation. Although the outcome was not what she had originally desired, she maintained her credibility as a physician leader.

So, what does this mean, and what does it say to you? There is a significant body of research regarding the developmental process that is relevant to your work as a leader.[3] Once again, let's remember that despite our preferences and hopes, the human developmental process does not occur in a linear manner. While incremental advancement is the goal of each coaching encounter, this expectation must be tempered.

Most people develop in a step-like rather than a direct linear manner. In other words, they have a burst of progress followed by a plateau. The plateau may extend for some time, followed by another advancement and eventual plateau. As this pattern continues, we encourage you to focus on overall development rather than idealistic continuity.

As we saw with Michael, there may even be points of regression where it appears that your target physician is taking two steps forward and one step back. This is normal and expected, especially when we are addressing behaviors that have been ingrained (and sometimes unaddressed) over several years.

Leaders do not want the target physician to overly lament or beat themselves up over what seems to be regressive backsliding, especially when they can see it and name it. In fact, the admission of backsliding can be a wonderful coaching opening. Asking questions such as, "What went wrong?" and "What could you have done differently?" deepen learning. Further asking, "Is there any relationship repair that you need to do as a result of this regression?" and "What adjustments will you make to help you get a better outcome in the future?" is action-oriented and easily translatable into expectations. As you no doubt recognize, we are grasping the opening and applying post-mortem thinking. In this regard, Jocelyn excelled.

Of course, we want the overall developmental process to be trending upward. This can be nuanced, especially when we are dealing with a struggling physician's behavior that demands immediate improvement. We must balance our knowledge of the development process with our need for tangible change.

THE NEXT BEST STEP

Coaching is a gentle dance. Physician leaders listen, summarize, reflect, probe, and encourage target physicians to stretch their awareness and thinking. Further, it is important that each meeting concludes with a commitment to developmental progress. There should be a next step or next best step, even if that step appears a bit limited. The important thing is that the step is one the target physician can commit to taking.

As noted above, we recommend asking three questions to ensure commitment to action. From a behavioral perspective, these questions help encourage target physicians to be accountable for their own growth and progress.[96] First, ask the target physician, "What will you do differently?" It is important here to emphasize action over intention. "I'll try to include my staff more" means nothing. "I will have a Friday morning team meeting each week" connotes action. In short, target physicians must determine and specify their changes. You may also ask the follow-up question, "When will you do it?" to solidify commitment.

The second question that is posed to target physicians drills in more deeply. Ask them, "Can you see yourself actually taking the actions you have specified?" This question forwards the action.

The third question begins to frame a way of thinking. Here, leaders can ask their targets, "If you take this action, what is likely to happen, and how will you deal with it?" The anticipatory nature of this question helps the target physician think through a range of possible reactions. Further, this style of *anticipatory thinking* is a skill that many target physicians need to develop, especially given their lagging skills of emotional intelligence. Recognize that these questions squarely put the ball in the target physician's court, where they maintain control — another characteristic of their behavior that we can use here to our advantage.

We need to dig deeper here. Let's assume that a target physician, Beth, has decided to meet with her PA, Jerry, to address some concerns that have prompted frustration and anger. Many complications and considerations can come into play. It's the leader's responsibility, in their coaching role, to move beyond the immediate action (meeting with Jerry) and help Beth engage in relevant anticipatory thinking.

"When will you meet with Jerry?" While that question is basic, it carries an impact. For example, Beth decided to tack this discussion on at the end of their regularly scheduled weekly meeting — a 30-minute exchange that was usually packed with discussion points. With only gentle questioning, the leader can help Beth recognize that a special meeting with only a single agenda item is probably best. She may also decide that having the meeting toward the end of the day makes sense, since both she and Jerry are less likely to be distracted or focused on other issues.

Next, help Beth anticipate Jerry's likely response using a *probability-risk analysis*. This can take many forms, but the following is illustrative. "What's the worst thing that can happen?" Beth may reflect that Jerry could become defensive and dismissive — actions well within his behavioral repertoire. "What's the probability this will occur?" Beth reasoned that this response was unlikely if she handled the communication properly. This, of course, leads to a consideration of the nature of the communication approach. Finally, a plan can be designed that carries a very low risk of matters going badly. This is the direction that Beth needs, and her willingness and confidence to engage Jerry in a difficult conversation should grow.

The corollary to anticipatory thinking is the *post-mortem review*. Here, the leader may encourage Beth to consider one additional task. "After meeting with Jerry, pull back and review how the meeting went. I'll be interested in your report back about what went well, what went poorly, and what you will do differently next time." This is how we learn, and it is a practice that most physicians who display disruptive behaviors need to embrace and develop.

Of course, it is likely that the plan of action and recurring work between the physician leader and the target physician will not go as smoothly as desired. In the next chapter, we will examine some common sticking points and offer ideas and approaches for working through each obstacle.

SUMMARY CHECKLIST

- Work with target physicians to develop a plan of action that addresses the issues of concern and places responsibility on the target physician.
- Be sure the plan of action includes immediate goals, action steps needed to achieve the stated goals, target completion dates, process of evaluating progress, and adjustments following evaluation.
- Establish clear consequences — ramifications that will be taken if goal progress falls short. As much as you can, gear the ramifications to matters that are important to the target physician with whom you are working.
- Escalate ramifications (consequences) sequentially. Clearly delineate each possible action and be sure the target physician is clear on the path of consequences.
- Have the courage to carry through and enact ramifications as necessary. Doing so is important for your credibility and the team's sense of equity.

CHAPTER 8

Areas for Growth

···

PHYSICIANS WHO DISPLAY DISRUPTIVE BEHAVIORS need guardrails, and they need clear consequences that encourage and motivate change. When disruptions become egregious and chronic, boundaries and immediate corrective actions are even more significant. In the face of these demands, physician leaders are challenged to take action.

In the previous two chapters, we outlined a recommended *process* — steps to take when meeting with target physicians and moving them to action. In this chapter, we consider specific areas of improvement for target physicians — the likely *content* of your conversations and ongoing support.

As physician leaders, you have the opportunity to help target physicians develop skills and behaviors that enhance their capacity to thrive as productive members of the clinical team. We explore some of the most critical needs target physicians are likely to face, and we stress how progressive physician leaders can help physicians move from being disgruntled irritants to flourishing and supportive colleagues. Again, we assert that this is part of the leader's charge: to help people become better versions of themselves.

Of course, as we noted previously, this lofty vision is complicated as leaders work with physicians who may be angry, defensive, and resentful that they are being singled out for attention. After all, they are talented physicians doing important, life-altering work.

The unfortunate bottom line is that you are seeking to work with and help people who may resist your help. Eye rolls, distorted facial expressions, and dismissive body language signal their disregard. Their responses can be terse and filled with sarcasm, suggesting a belief that their valuable time and talent are being wasted. Physician leaders must fight the natural tendency to veer from the high road, and they must be cautious not to engage in a destructive tit-for-tat exchange.

We recognize that target physicians may not want the developmental help that their leaders can provide. Here, it is important to step back and take a long-run view. It's not hyperbolic to suggest that physician leaders may be acting to save a career — a consideration that is especially significant for younger target physicians who have yet to alienate their colleagues and staff.

A FOUNDATIONAL PERSPECTIVE

Before outlining specific areas of improvement that may be at play with target physicians, we consider a foundational perspective that flows through virtually all areas of focus for the target physician. As we noted previously, based on our training and experience, we have found more success when adopting the position that adding a behavior is simpler and more easily accepted than stopping or decreasing a behavior.

For instance, when working with someone who is seen as too direct and curt, we encourage them to develop a more balanced approach to others by engaging with curiosity about others' perspectives and experiences rather than working toward "being less direct."

In many cases, one of the behaviors we work with target physicians to change is their ability to make and accept "bids for connection," or verbal attempts to connect with other people.[136] Research on the importance of warmth in leadership effectiveness tells us that a building block of the target physician's development plan should be to engage in basic interpersonal connections.[137]

Using our foundational perspective, we suggest target physicians start by adding simple acts of connection, such as addressing their colleagues by their names. We may also encourage them to smile more often or offer sincere personal appreciation or recognition for the good work that is done.

We often work with target physicians to show sincere appreciation. We emphasize that statements of recognition should be specific, calling out the behavior that is being recognized and the ways the person being recognized carried it out. In sum, we encourage specific feedback that is geared to the recipient.

Consider an example. We asked Dale if he regularly thanked his team for their work in the OR. "I always do," Dale replied, confident that he'd nailed this query. When we asked how he expressed his thanks, Dale was clear. "I say, 'Thanks, team; thanks for your help with this surgery'."

We encouraged Dale and noted that such feedback was quite important. Yet, we pressed further, noting that while such global affirmation was important, individualized affirmation could (and should) be added. Perhaps Jane, one of his OR nurses, may benefit from feeling appreciated in a more personal way. It need not be over-the-top or time-consuming. "Jane, that was a complicated procedure. You really stepped up. You made a real difference." That's it.

Note that we began by pointing out Dale's instinct to say "thank you." We started from what he was already in the habit of doing. But pay attention to what was added. First, Jane received affirmation — which we all need and receive far too infrequently. Second, by asserting that Jane made a difference, Dale was tapping into Jane's need for significance — the feeling that she is important and needed. In fact, we argue that this sense of personal significance is one of the most powerful motivators that affects each of us. Third, the entire conversation, short as it may be, has a reinforcing tone. It indicates good work and progress toward helping others, thus encouraging and motivating further positive and helping behaviors.[138] Fourth, none of this takes much time, and none of it requires target physicians to extend themselves too much.

Over time, small shifts in communication patterns such as those outlined above change the tone of interactions and the perceptions others have about the target physician's intentions. There is another reality. When leaders use such positive affirmations consistently and authentically, they build trust, and others are more likely to dismiss or minimize an occasional errant comment or problematic behavior. When communication is enhanced and made more personal, others are more likely to focus on positives over negatives.

In our example, you may recognize a theme: emotional intelligence. Indeed, most physicians who have been referred to us as a result of their disruptive behavior have been asked to make changes in the areas of self-awareness, self-management, other awareness, and relationship management. This is emotional intelligence in alignment with the model put forth by Daniel Goleman.[139] It is often defined as "the ability to accurately perceive your own and others' emotions; to understand the signals that emotions send about relationships; and to manage your own and others' emotions."[140]

In this chapter, we discuss how you might work with your target physician in four key areas where they are likely to be deficient: self-awareness, impulse control (an aspect of self-management), empathy (other-awareness), and apologies (relationship management). All of these areas will help the target physician build and, in some cases, rebuild trust. Let's explore each.

ENHANCING SELF-AWARENESS

Target physicians likely have low levels of self-awareness, which Goleman and colleagues assert is the foundation of emotional intelligence.[89]

Accordingly, developmental coaching often begins with an assessment of the target physician's self-awareness and then a decision: Is a degree of self-awareness established such that we can build from accepted strengths and weaknesses? Or, must we help target physicians develop a keener sense of self-awareness? Without self-awareness, target physicians are unlikely to fully and meaningfully address developmental issues unless there is a perception of underlying needs. Without awareness, there is usually no deep, committed developmental action.

In her research, Tasha Eurich segmented self-awareness into two categories. The first category, internal self-awareness, "represents how clearly we see our own values, passions, aspirations, fit with our environment's reactions (including thoughts, feelings, behaviors, strengths, and weaknesses), and impact on others."[141]

The second category, external self-awareness, pinpoints how others see us regarding the factors noted above.[141] Evidence indicates that when people are aware of how others see them (high levels of external self-awareness), they are likely to display empathy toward and appreciation for others and their points of view.[141]

Of course, it is challenging to help target physicians become aware of what they have historically failed to recognize. Indeed, their initial response is likely to be one of denial — disagreeing and dismissing perspectives contrary to their well-honed self-image. Here, we suggest two possible ideas or approaches.

First, one may use 360-degree assessments to offer the physician feedback. The strength of these assessments is their provision of data and evidence. Although the evidence is drawn from the perceptions and impressions of others, when the feedback is consistent across respondents, a cumulative effect is present. In other words, the force of the evidence becomes hard to summarily dismiss.

However promising 360-degree assessments may be, we encourage caution here. First, staff may be reluctant to offer honest responses. Even with the protection of anonymity, they may fear broad retaliation from the target physician — a fear that may have a reasonable base.

Second, unless the assessment is part of an overall assessment for the entire unit, target physicians will rightly feel singled out, thereby reinforcing negative labels.

Third, assessments are costly, especially when conducted unit-wide. They can be useful, but only when the above caveats are weighed.

Because of these concerns, we typically suggest a second approach. Here, you define for the target physician a glimpse of reality — clear statements of how others view them. This can be tricky, and it rests on careful explanations that protect the confidentiality of those who have given feedback.

For example, you may address a target physician (Bob) this way: "Bob, when you are frustrated, you are seen by others as harsh, angry, and diminishing of others." You must move slowly to allow the target physician to absorb and process what you just said.

It is likely that you will hear a counter-response that deflects or excuses the perceptions you just noted. Allow the target physician to have their say by listening without offering counter-arguments. Now comes the key. "Bob, I'm not saying you are a harsh, angry, and dismissive person. I am saying that when others interact with you, they describe your behavior as harsh, angry, and dismissive." Again, take a few moments for the statement to settle in.

Maintain the focus on behavior and impressions associated with that behavior. You may also explore intentions here. "Bob, what is the impression you intend to leave with people?" When this gap is surfaced, leaders can press on, probing in a reflective manner that encourages joint exploration, identification, and insight. "Bob, can you think of what behaviors on your part may lead others to feel you are being harsh, angry, or dismissive?"

Physician leaders should convey to target physicians that both parties are working together to identify behaviors that produce something other than the intended impact. This exercise not only builds self-awareness for the particular concern being discussed but also provides a framework that may be helpful in cultivating even more self-awareness going forward.

IMPULSE CONTROL

Next, physician leaders may need to help their target physicians explore the cloudy territory of *emotional regulation* — what we typically refer to as *impulse control*. Stated succinctly, impulse control is "the ability to resist or delay an impulse, drive, or temptation to act … or to react appropriately without uncontrolled anger."[142] Here, most experts support a cascading model, where self-awareness must precede impulse control.[143] In other words, you must be self-aware before you can engage in self-management.

The logic here is obvious. When one becomes aware of the emergence and rising intensity of their emotions, especially while they are occurring, they have a better chance of regulating or controlling an impulse to lash out in a rage of emotional intensity.

The key is for the target physician to become aware of early signals or internal cues – those early signs of frustration or disappointment which, if unchecked, will escalate and emerge as angry or hostile responses. We've helped target physicians reflect on past circumstances to surface these triggers and to monitor themselves closely in situations where they have become angry or hostile. Their growing awareness of early signals allows them to put on the brakes and take action to remove themselves from the situation, short-circuit the reaction by diverting attention from the explosive emotion, and ultimately engage in a more positive response.

Again, an example may be useful. Like many of you, we find ourselves in too many unstructured and rambling meetings. As time slips by and little appears to be accomplished, we can feel ourselves beginning to experience the early tinges of anxiety and frustration. Unchecked, those emotions escalate, springing forth in a stinging commentary we wish could be recanted as soon as it is spoken.

The key — the magic — is to thwart those emotions from escalating by sensing the early signals and deciding on an appropriate reaction. Often, one of us responds to cues by writing down what they are thinking of saying. Not surprisingly, seeing it in writing often provides perspective on how the comments would be received and perceived, and discretion can prevail accordingly.

At times, the diversion can be subtle. For example, we worked with Elle, a physician who readily admitted that she was repeatedly becoming frustrated with Linda, one of her PAs. Elle explained to us, "Every time I correct Linda, she runs to HR, claiming that I am angrily yelling at her. I'm correcting her and doing so firmly. But I can't see why she always thinks I'm mad and yelling." There is gold here and an angle for further and deeper discussion.

In this situation, we encouraged Elle to label and explain her emotions as a prelude to her corrective comments. "Linda, I'm frustrated, and I'm concerned about the patient you were with. I expect you to respond when the patient's numbers hit that threshold. Do you understand?" Hopefully, Linda will recognize that frustration, concern, and clarity of expectations are the emotional elements Elle is expressing rather than anger.

There is another advantage to personally labeling one's emotions: it is a diversion that increases self-awareness. For Elle, labeling emotions is a reminder that she must be careful with her tone and the force of her delivery, thereby minimizing the prospect of being seen as angry and yelling.

Another straightforward statement may be helpful to share with target physicians. Remind them that "you do not have to say everything you think." Hopefully, target physicians will learn to judiciously read the people and the situation, determining that some comments are best left unspoken.

These are very small steps, but this is the path to progress, improvement, and lasting change. Importantly, it helps the target physician focus on what they can do rather than on what needs to be stopped or avoided.

In other cases, there may be a deeper reason for helping the target physician delve into self-awareness and impulse control. Sometimes, the target physician's self-awareness has been clouded by self-deception or delusion.[144] They may have created a version of reality that places them as the patient-centric hero, brighter than others and fighting systemic mediocrity to unleash their special talents to ensure top-level outcomes. The physician leader's job is not to argue with them regarding these lofty self-appraisals; rather, the leader's job is to help target physicians see other versions of events — versions that are being experienced by others and much more consistent with evidence-based reality.

In cases where you feel as if you are challenging the target physician's very identity, recognize that you may also be creating a state of cognitive dissonance for the target physician since evidence is presented that contradicts their self-concept.[145] Generally, dissonance creates an aversive motivational state, prompting the holder to reduce disparities and attain a more comfortable condition of cognitive consistency. Of course, one way to reduce the dissonance is to dismiss or discredit any information that runs counter to one's self-concept. Indeed, target physicians often take this approach.

However, when enough consistent evidence is presented, we hope that unequivocal rejection is an unacceptable alternative, especially for bright and talented people. Unable to easily reject claims, target physicians, we hope, will begin to unravel the dissonance by making changes in their personal behavior. Let's be careful not to trivialize the intensity of these behavioral dynamics. Considerable processing is taking place. Rejecting conflicting evidence can be the easiest path.

BUILDING EMPATHY

While self-awareness is foundational to emotional intelligence, other-awareness can be just as critical to develop, particularly as the target physician may be grappling to understand the perspective of those who have been negatively affected by their behavior. Here, we emphasize the interpersonal skill of *empathy*. Cambridge professor Simon Baren-Cohen suggests that empathy is "the ability to identify what someone else is thinking or feeling and to respond to that person's thoughts and feelings with an appropriate emotion."[146] For target physicians, the capacity for empathy is clouded by a strong *commitment bias*, a dominating belief in and reliance on one's established perspectives and points of view.[147]

How can physician leaders help target physicians become more empathetic? Once again, we turn to the pioneering work of Daniel Goleman as he helps us understand that empathy is really about reaching toward and focusing on others. He further asserts that empathetic behaviors (skills) can be learned, developed, and enhanced.[148]

Helen Riess of Massachusetts General Hospital notes that building physician empathy begins with engagement with others — initiating small actions like positive facial expressions (smiling), making appropriate eye contact, and paying attention to other's expressions and body language.[149]

Beyond these ideas, we encourage physician leaders to help target physicians focus on two fundamental skills: *engaged listening* and *reflective summarizing*. Although these themes may require a bit of a stretch for some physicians, these skills can be practiced and enhanced with focused attention.

Engaged listening rests on the tenet that people like to believe that others are listening to and considering what they are saying — attuning to their comments and seeking to understand the points they are making and the needs behind them.[89] We encourage physician leaders to remind their target physicians of an important behavioral theme: when others push back and make demands, it generally signals some level of unmet needs.[150]

Trying to recognize underlying needs rather than merely focusing on the immediate words being spoken takes attention, and it takes some time to reframe events from the perspectives of others. Encourage target physicians to probe for understanding — perhaps simply using the basic interpersonal retort, "Help me understand."[151] Asking others for help understanding why issues are so important opens a window to awareness and signals others of concern and attention.

These basic steps alone, when taken over time, change perceptions. They signal an intention to engage in *other-focused interactions* — the foundation of projecting empathy.

Reflective summarizing is a powerful tool for building and establishing perceptions of empathy. As explained in a previous book, "the reflective summary response occurs as we reflect back or express to the other party what we have just heard and learned."[14] It need not be extensive: "Nancy, if I am hearing you correctly, you are concerned about two important points – the workload of your nurses and their reluctance to shift from one doctor's team to another. Is that right?"

Such reflections signal listening, processing, and concern. They also prompt continued communications. Note that reflective summaries do not connote agreement; they are expressions of thoughtfulness and understanding — again, helping reformulate others' impressions of target physicians.

For target physicians, displaying occasional empathic activities is less important than presenting *consistency* — engaging in genuine communications and empathetic actions across situations and across time. Consistency will be strained by the pressures of time and the demands of stressful situations that will always arise.

In many ways, there is wisdom in understanding that others interpret the true intentions of target physicians most deeply and clearly through the physician's responses when they are under pressure.[152] In other words, others feel that true intentions are revealed through behaviors exhibited in the midst of adversity and crisis. Simply bringing these points to the attention of target physicians is surely insufficient. Yet, they are seeds, and the points can be reinforced as physician leaders interact and coach target physicians.

Ultimately, improving empathy should begin with small steps. Although some points may seem inconsequential, when combined, a powerful message emerges. Let's restate some key behaviors: Start by encouraging target physicians to address colleagues by name. Greet them. Smile. Make eye contact. Encourage them to ask questions that recognize that their colleagues have real lives beyond their clinical roles. Help them see that only 20 or 30 seconds of other-focused "small talk" can convey personal empathy.[119]

You may also suggest that showing appreciation for others can be as simple as heartfelt thanks, as we pointed out in the example of Dale. Encourage them to tell colleagues that they are valued, important, and significant players in the overall effort to deliver top-quality healthcare. Again, these recognitions need not be overdone, nor do they need to be time-consuming. The key is that others are addressed in warm, specific, personal tones that convey their significance and contribution. The words are important, but the sincerity behind the words is even more important in affecting others' perceptions.

APOLOGIES

The target physician's initial behavioral manifestation of empathy is often an apology. But, when apologies are delivered after weeks (if not months or years) of dismissive or disrespectful interactions, it is reasonable for their teammates to feel the apologies lack depth and sincerity. As such, they are merely an expression of words that do little to change the dynamics. In some cases, apologies may be further discounted when the actions for which apologies are made continue.

We recently worked with a physician leader who was navigating ongoing tension between two of his physicians. Cal seemed to have a special knack for diminishing Lakshmi, often questioning her professional skills. Never shy, Cal made sure his colleagues (and even some residents) were aware of his concerns about Lakshmi's clinical competency.

The two would have tense exchanges, marked by Cal's sarcastic and cutting comments — behaviors that were clearly over-the-top and out of line. Interestingly, after many of these exchanges, Cal appeared contrite and offered either an in-person or emailed apology.

At first, Lakshmi accepted these apologies. However, despite the apologies, Cal's actions showed no sign of changing. When we met, Lakshmi was firm that she had no desire to accept any further apologies from Cal. "He says he's sorry, but nothing changes. The apology means nothing — just another form of trying to dominate and minimize me."

When encouraging target physicians to apologize to those they have offended, we suggest a three-step model. First, the apologizer needs to be clear and specific regarding the actions for which they are apologizing. Further, they need to admit that the action was unfair, unkind, or unprofessional. In other words, they must take responsibility for what they have done.

Accordingly, a blanket apology, such as "Lakshmi, I'm sorry," is insufficient. Situational detail and responsibility are necessary. "Lakshmi, yesterday, when I argued with you in front of colleagues, I asserted that your idea was stupid. That was unfair. I was frustrated, but my response was inappropriate. I want to apologize for my words and actions."

The second step in an effective apology is to explain behavioral intentions for the future. "Lakshmi, I know you are talented. I also know that you and I have different ways of doing things. In the future, when I disagree, I will do so privately, hoping we can talk through the issues and reach an agreement. I will not drag colleagues or staff into the fray." Lakshmi now has a statement of commitment — a recognition of what was wrong and a promise to rectify the offense going forward.

The third step is most critical. Over time, Cal must keep his commitments. By doing so, the apology has meaning, and trust can be rebuilt. An apology that is not confirmed through reformative behavior does little more than create frustration and further erode trust, which brings us to the last aspect of working with the target physicians that we see most often.

REBUILDING TRUST

One common outcome of target physicians' disruptive behaviors is a breach of trust between them and the rest of the staff. As physician leaders work with target physicians, it is important to help them (1) understand that a breach has arisen, (2) recognize the impact and ramifications of the breach, and (3) help them take steps to rebuild trust. It's likely that the target physician will challenge the leader's assessment of broken trust relationships.

Prolonged discussion and debate over whether or not a breach of trust has arisen are frequently non-productive. Instead, focus on the fact that others perceive, believe, and feel like trust has been broken. Before delving further into specifics, let's look at trust — its meaning and its effect.

Research from Frei and Morriss and from Zenger and Folkman have established four foundations of trust.[153,154] The first foundational factor is *authenticity*, an assessment that one is sincere and that others are interacting with the real person. Second is *logic*, drawn from perceptions that one's decisions are based on sound reasoning and judgment. Third is the factor of *empathy*, demonstrating genuine regard for others and caring about their well-being and their success. Fourth is *consistency*, which emphasizes maintaining parity between commitments (promises) and subsequent action.

Note how these four factors are interwoven within the emotional intelligence dimensions and examples we've already provided. No matter the presenting problem you find yourself discussing with the target physician, eroded trust is likely a concurrent concern.

Perceptions of factors like *authenticity* and *logic* are complex and difficult to reasonably assess and alter. Further, *logic* is generally not the primary concern with target physicians. Accordingly, while we do not dismiss the power of these factors, we suggest beginning with the factors of *empathy* and *consistency*.

Trust is also affected by *perceptions of intention*. For example, if others believe that a physician's underlying intention is one of an other-focused drive to be helpful and secure the best possible patient outcomes, some degree of latitude may be tolerated. However, if others feel that the physician's underlying intent is self-focused, seeking recognition, building bases of power, and other forms of self-aggrandizement, trust dynamics are resting on unsteady ground.

Of course, the path to rebuilding trust is complicated by history. Trust is built and rebuilt from actions, established incrementally over time. Trust is enhanced when one shows consistency between words and actions. Trust grows as one is seen by others as understanding and accepting individual differences and working in a positive way to support others' growth and development.[155] And, most importantly, trust is a two-way street.

While you will want to surface concerns about trust and work with the target physician to rebuild it, you may also need to work closely with the rest of the team as well. We discuss this in more detail in the next chapter.

SUMMARY CHECKLIST

As a physician leader, you may perceive that the themes above are also valuable when interacting with all physicians. Indeed. Further, by doing so, physician leaders are modeling appropriate and effective interactive behaviors for their target physicians. Below are takeaways that can be helpful in your own approach, in addition to suggestions you may make to the target physician.

- Find ways to add positive behaviors rather than simply stopping negative ones.
- Use emotional intelligence as a helpful sense-making framework, investigating and encouraging development in areas such as self-awareness, impulse control, empathy, and relationship management.
- Consider tools like 360-degree feedback as a means to self-awareness, but direct, compassionate communication often can help target physicians better understand others' perceptions.
- Enhance impulse control by recognizing early emotional signals that can help prevent outbursts and promote more thoughtful interactions.
- Cultivate empathy and encourage effective apologies.

CHAPTER 9

The Rest of the Team

$\mathcal{S}$OMEWHAT SURPRISINGLY, one of the most important aspects of supporting the development of target physicians is managing the narrative, expectations, and encouragement of their peers. In other words, one facet of leading the team is helping with performance challenges and facilitating the professional development of its members. If we were writing a book for a leader in a traditional corporate environment, we would point you directly to well-researched aspects of effective teams: shared vision, roles and norms, and psychological safety.

But, first, let's normalize that these models may always leave physician leaders feeling a little uncertain, a little tentative. You see, most team leadership literature assumes that leaders inhabit a well-defined role that is different from that of the team members, with more authority and agency. However, in many cases, physician leaders are partners in their practice and are responsible for RVU production and contract fulfillment that does not differ from that of other peers. While leaders may receive some compensation and protected time for administrative duties, the formal administrative role often provides only marginal increases in authority.

Instead, as in traditional academic environments, physician leaders are often called to engage in what is called *transcollegial leadership*, defined as: "the process involved in leaders systematically, but informally, relating to persons and groups of equivalent authority...for the advancement of its mission not for personal gain."[17]

So, while leading collaboratively *across* units in the hospital or healthcare system by virtue of your appointment, influencing your peers to put aside self-interest and personal gain must occur without a great deal of additional vertical or formal authority. Rather, you'll need to make the case that your expectations will lead to optimum results for people based on their values. And their values may vary widely, along with other disruptions to rational self-interest such as mood, personality, and self-evaluations.[156]

For instance, as a leader, you may sit on a committee that includes other physicians, nurses, pharmacists, and quality improvement staff, all brought together to reduce falls as patients recover from surgery. Working collaboratively, the committee develops a comprehensive, mission-aligned plan that includes implementing standardized fall risk assessments for all surgical patients, developing personalized prevention plans, and enhancing patient education.

But there is a complication. The physicians in your practice have a reputation for discharging patients quickly after surgery, and the length of hospital stay has been a KPI since before you came on board. You are hesitant to pilot the program within your department, given the interests of your fellow physicians, but you also know that the initiative is an important aspect of the hospital system's overall quality initiative.

Continuous improvement like this requires transcollegial leadership, as does managing the team through distressed physician behavior that has been escalated to the hospital or system level.

Relative to the topic of engaging with target physicians, your *organizational* leadership role may call you to engage with hospital or system leadership, the Human Resources Department, or other stakeholders in ways that mitigate risks created by the target physician, ideally by improving their performance and interpersonal relationships. However, your role as a *team* leader may rely on influence and collaboration rather than authority.

This may be beneficial, given that you'll need longer-term commitment and dedication rather than short-term compliance in order to manage interpersonal disruptions and the long-term endeavor of team cohesion, as discussed in Chapter 3. But, unlike leaders in traditional organizations, you can't rely on compliance on your way to commitment. You can't easily put mandates in place when it comes to how team members treat each other. While this makes your task more difficult, the influence you'll need to use also makes for a larger payoff when it comes to team effectiveness.

WINNING TEAMS

Before we turn our attention to the key points you'll need to keep in mind when it comes to managing your team through the process of the target physician's development, let's review some key aspects of successful teams. Regardless of how the *leadership* of teams may differ, team researchers generally agree that the effectiveness of teams should be evaluated on two dimensions: performance and viability.

Performance is context-specific and is often a more intuitively understood leadership role. You can influence performance significantly by articulating a clear vision and direction for the team, outlining its purpose, goals, and objectives — being a key contributor to the health and well-being of your community by providing responsive and high-quality care. By providing a compelling vision, leaders inspire team members to pursue common goals such as RVU production, quality, patient experience, and so on. It is also critical to ensure that every team member understands their role in achieving these goals and how their contributions add to the overall success of the team.

Teams also must remain viable; that is, they must be affectively and cognitively willing to work with one another again. Viability rests upon open communication and collaboration among team members, creating an environment of transparency, mutual respect, and trust.

In teams, trust between individual members certainly contributes to viability. But, even when team membership changes or the team encounters a new challenge, strong team norms surrounding reliability and respect may be a proxy for the type of trust that results in team viability.

While you may not be in a position to choose the team or lead one through its initial developmental stages, the Tuckman model[157] of team formation can facilitate your understanding of how to foster performance and viability. Additionally, this model serves as a reasonable diagnostic to help leaders determine how they can intervene to improve team effectiveness.

At the outset, the group is in the *forming* stage, understanding expectations of their work together and the skills and competencies available through its members. They may also become aware of the collective workload required and the implications for their individual workload. They may be particularly attuned to equity in workload, although team members may be willing to overlook potential inequities until the next stage is reached. For example, the call responsibilities of a newly restructured team may be apparent, but how individual call schedules will be divided and negotiated may not yet be determined.

At this stage, task performance is the focus, although as they begin their work, the team starts to test their assumptions about the task and the individual team members' contributions. The ways in which the team members will work together become more important, and viability becomes more of a priority.

As the team members continue to work together, they enter the *storming* stage. While the name suggests this is a time of conflict, it doesn't have to be. In this stage, the team members voice opinions and deepen the level of vulnerability-based trust.

According to Patrick Lencioni in his book *The Five Dysfunctions of a Team*,[158] vulnerability-based trust goes beyond the transactional level of trust, the belief that the person will do what they say they will do. It even goes beyond the awareness of team members' backgrounds and working styles, and it transcends the implicit status differences and hierarchies that can be present in healthcare teams.

Rather, vulnerability-based trust is seen in the behaviors of the person extending trust: they ask for help, are willing to take risks (even if that means being wrong), and contribute to the development of their teammates. A closely related concept, *psychological safety*, will be discussed later as a key aspect of your role in the repair of relationships damaged by disruptive behavior.

In the storming stage, team members may disagree and engage in discussions about expectations they have of one another, and a structure to their work begins to form. The leader can clarify roles, responsibilities, and expectations to reduce potential sources of conflict and keep the team focused on common objectives.

Yet, the way the team engages in productive conflict is also critical to its growing viability. Successfully navigating this stage and arriving at a consensus about shared leadership and accountability solidifies trust, making viability an outcome of the work in this stage. A key outcome of this stage is structure — a structure that supports team performance.

As the team moves toward their first successful performance together, even one step in a larger project or endeavor, they enter the *norming* stage. It is here that an effective team engages in feedback and reflection sessions to assess their progress, identify areas for improvement, and establish the expectation of regular feedback and continuous improvement.

This also can be a time of celebration and confidence-building, as well as the acceptance of team members. The team toggles back to the priority of performance, and the realization (often made explicit by the leader) that the team's collective effort was critical enhances viability.

At its most effective, the team is in the *performing* stage. It has established valuable norms and ways of working, fortified by strong relationships among team members. The team continues to perform effectively, which reinforces viability, builds team efficacy, and amplifies accomplishments.

Jon Katzenbach and Douglas Smith suggest that a high-performing team goes far beyond baseline performance and viability. A high-performing team is one in which the team can succeed or fail as a whole; individual performance becomes secondary.[159] This motivates individual team members to support one another's highest performance in addition to performing at their own highest levels. While your team may not have that degree of interdependence, supporting one another's performance is desirable when helping a physician move past distress and back into a cohesive team.

The role of the leader of a newly formed team is to shepherd the group through the four stages by providing information and structure in the early stages, as well as reflecting, articulating, and celebrating team success in the later stages. In reality, physician leaders seldom lead newly formed teams; however, even in intact teams, leaders need to monitor the team's disintegration and reformation over and over again. This is true not only when new members are welcomed to the team but also when team conflict (such as that brought on by the behaviors of a distressed physician) arises.

One key aspect of managing the team's restoration process is supporting and facilitating trust repair, which ensures the team can maintain the levels of viability and performance it has earned. In the day-to-day rush of most busy healthcare environments, people may breach trust. One definition of trust suggests that it is the "intention to accept vulnerability based upon positive expectations of the intentions or behavior of another."[108]

For example, asking the physician a question about applying best practice to patient care (which suggests a lack of knowledge and, therefore, vulnerability) may result in a hasty response (at best), or an angry reprimand about challenging the physician's approach. Ensuring that the team has opportunities to repair trust through verbal statements, apologies, or building the reservoir of vulnerability-based trust,[160] and modeling repair behavior are important aspects of team leadership.

We have been talking about teams and the presence of a distressed physician in the abstract. At this point, it may be helpful to consider an example.

Several years ago, we worked with Rajesh, a physician who had been referred to coaching as a requirement of his performance improvement plan. Raj is a skilled and experienced physician, and he has been a valuable member of his practice for many years. In the months before we met him, however, he had become disenchanted with the hospital system's response to financial difficulties and resented some of the restrictions it placed on his ability to care for patients with the most cutting-edge equipment and techniques. As a result, he became prone to outbursts of anger and frustration, especially during high-stress situations such as emergency surgeries or when dealing with difficult patients. His colleagues witnessed him raising his voice at nurses and other staff members, and there were reports of derogatory remarks made in front of patients and their families.

Initially, as predicted, Raj was defensive and insisted that his behavior was justified given the circumstances. He downplayed the impact of his actions on the team dynamics and patient care, arguing that he is simply passionate about providing the best possible medical care despite the financial limitations of the hospital.

But, after several meetings and the realization that his treatment of team members was counter to his value of providing excellent care, Raj began to see the disconnect between his intentions and their impact. Through his own commitment to personal development and excellence, Raj began to make positive changes. Not only did he focus on responding rather than reacting in stressful circumstances, but he also made several bids for connection, attempting to repair trust and demonstrate his eagerness to move through the team disruption caused by his behavior.

Emily, the medical director for surgical services (who was not a member of Raj's practice), was supportive of him and his development. She met with him weekly to track progress on his performance improvement plan and was generally positive (though not particularly encouraging or forthcoming) about changes she had seen in his relationships with the surgical team. However, despite his improvements, she continued to get negative feedback from the team, and she seemed to be focused on his shortcomings rather than his progress.

As this continued, we pressed Raj for his own perceptions of his performance instead of relying upon those of the medical director, helping him mine for positive reinforcement that keeps motivation high and rebuilds his sense of identity as a valued team member.

While Raj felt good about how he had rebuilt relationships with three of the five physicians in their small practice, other team members were less inclusive. The two newest partners had been friends since medical school and had courted Raj for his vote in the past when a majority was needed. However, recently, they had started actively excluding Raj. It felt isolating and made it difficult for Raj to focus on his role in meetings. The nurses and other staff members attempted to ignore the issue, which made Raj feel as if they didn't see him genuinely attempting to improve.

When we asked what might be leading to the negative feedback, Raj couldn't think of anything specific; rather, he felt he was being treated the same despite the changes he'd made in his behavior and outlook. He sometimes overheard whispers and disparaging remarks, but he was determined to remain positive. He understood that repairing trust takes time, and he was committed to his team.

But, the isolation continued, and Raj became hypervigilant in his interactions. He eventually began to second guess his decisions and expect rejection and criticism. His sense of competence and confidence were repeatedly challenged, which led to his resorting again to expressing anger and frustration.

This time, Raj realized he was not honoring his own values and providing the best care he possibly could. Ultimately, Raj left the practice and took a position in academic healthcare. While he is thriving in his new environment, Raj describes this experience — attempting to reintegrate with his team after his period of distress — as the low point of his career.

While we could not observe the interactions Raj described as he was attempting to regain his place as a valued member of both his practice and the hospital's medical team, we were not convinced that Emily had done all she could do as his leader. She held him accountable to his performance improvement plan, but she did not establish vulnerability-based trust that would be helpful in Raj's development.

By extension, we are unsure whether the team had the necessary trust, norms, or leadership that lead to high levels of team viability. And, we do not have evidence that Emily responded to team members' complaints about Raj by acknowledging their experience while also challenging them to support Raj in his development.

Emily's response to Raj and his team members did not create a sense of *psychological safety*, a concept developed by Amy Edmondson in her work with healthcare teams. Defined as "a shared belief held by members of a team that it is OK to take risks, express their ideas and concerns, to speak up with questions, and to admit mistakes,"[161] a psychologically safe environment is required for the target physician to learn new ways of interacting with members of their team.

Psychological safety is particularly important in healthcare teams, where status hierarchies may diminish the collaboration necessary for high-quality patient care.[48] The leader plays an important role in creating a sense of psychological safety in healthcare environments. As noted by Ingrid Marie Nembhard and Amy Edmondson in their study of NICU teams, "if a leader is democratic, supportive, and welcomes questions and challenges, team members are likely to feel greater psychological safety in the team and in their interactions with each other."[48]

Public and interpersonal behavior change involves risk on the part of the physician making the change, acceptance of past mistakes, and the clumsiness of learning on the part of those on the receiving end of the changes. Even if the target physician feels they can make significant changes, the extent to which they believe those changes will lead to the restoration of their perceived value to the team affects their motivation to engage and persist in change.

Emily's failure to challenge team members to give Raj a chance despite the risk of being disappointed compounded the problem. McKinsey and Company note that leaders who support and challenge team members create a *learning zone* where employees feel comfortable requesting help and offering it.[162]

Edmondson created a seven-item questionnaire to assess the perception of psychological safety.[161] It is clear how these beliefs affect some of the most consistent findings with regard to psychological safety (like innovation, engagement, and decision-making), but also how these beliefs create a positive environment for the target physician's development. In assessing the psychological safety of the team you lead, ask yourself if people on your team believe:

1. If you make a mistake on this team, it is not held against you.
2. Members of this team are able to bring up problems and tough issues.
3. People on this team accept others for being different.
4. It is safe to take a risk on this team.
5. It isn't difficult to ask other members of this team for help.
6. No one on this team would deliberately act in a way that undermines my efforts.
7. Working with members of this team, my unique skills and talents are valued and utilized.

From the target physician's perspective, the extent to which they believe people will accept them, continue to acknowledge and value their talents, allow them to fail as they learn different ways of interacting, and help them improve by bringing missteps to their attention is a key aspect of their ability to persist in making important changes.

In our example, we encouraged Raj to test these beliefs independent of Emily's impressions, and our conclusion is that he did not feel psychologically safe in his work team. In fact, he may have continued to be seen as the source of team problems, even those that he did not directly affect.

It is estimated that 25% of team conflicts are attributable to one person on the team.[163] While a physician who is making positive changes may not be disruptive, they still may be a scapegoat, subtly blamed for the problems of the team and conveniently serving as an excuse for other team members to avoid interrogating their own behavior.

The leader can positively influence this situation by modeling perspective-taking, asking questions of the target physician in team meetings when others are excluding them, displaying empathy, and surfacing insights about viability that can be valuable to the entire team.

In Raj's case, we might have recommended that Emily highlight her own developmental goals and challenges to progress in team meetings and thank the team for their patience. This may lead to a deeper conversation (in the same meeting or the next) about the developmental goals of each team member. It is important not to make Raj's challenges a team problem; this may lead to resentment and increased perceptual salience for the target physician. Hopefully, modeling compassion and appreciation for shortcomings can shift the team's perspective and set a tone of continuous interpersonal improvement.

Of course, we encourage leaders to invest in psychological safety and create a baseline level of trust among members before the team is faced with reintegrating a physician who is actively working to change their behavior. However, there are several reasons why that investment may not be sufficient.

For instance, you may be a new leader, taking over an embattled team. Workload and financial strain may diminish opportunities to build relationships and interact in a way that builds vulnerability-based trust. Or, it may not have occurred to you that ensuring psychological safety was a priority before circumstances like rehabilitating a physician's damaged team relationships presented themselves.

Project Aristotle, a large-scale investigation at Google that studied effective teams, concluded that who was on a team mattered less than how the team worked together.[161] No matter who is on your team, you can influence its effectiveness by investing in psychological safety.

But, if you are like Emily and you find yourself in a position to shepherd a distressed physician and their team through breaches of trust and respect on their way back to effectiveness, the first step is to recognize your responsibility in modeling and facilitating a psychologically safe environment.

When interacting with the team, make yourself accessible and open to concerns, but encourage a supportive and developmental environment for the target physician. Coach team members to give the target physician constructive feedback that is focused on behaviors and actions rather than personal attributes. This will empower team members and accelerate the positive change of the target physician.

You might also consider admitting your own mistakes and vulnerabilities, which reinforces a learning environment. Alongside this encouragement and support of all team members, leaders should also (re)set and (re)communicate clear expectations regarding behavior, communication norms, and accountability within the team. This helps establish a shared understanding of what constitutes acceptable behavior and further reinforces psychological safety.

TEAM LEADERSHIP

While encouraging the team to support the target physician, the physician leader must pay special attention to the rest of the team. Remember that they are likely to feel that they are being treated unfairly, likely asserting that equity has been breached. They surmise, perhaps appropriately, that the target physician is creating conditions that diminish the workplace, threaten morale, and negatively affect clinical outcomes.

Further, as we have noted previously, when the team feels that the leader is not addressing target physician issues appropriately, the confidence in and credibility of the physician leader is drawn into question, and complaints and criticisms rise.

The leader's approach here is tricky and nuanced. Confidential activities between the physician leader and the target physician must be maintained and protected. However, the team needs to know that the leader is not ignoring the situation. Those two themes, simple as they seem, are critical, and they must coincide. Interestingly, in the face of an informational underload, people often assume the bleakest of scenarios. Informational gaps are filled by assumptions and rumors. Here, team members are likely to believe that the leader is following the path of tolerance, and that path is perceived as blatantly unfair.

The rest of the team needs to know at least three things. First, they must understand that the leader is *aware* of the situation. Little is more damning for a leader than others' perceptions that they are acting with their head in the sand, oblivious to the turmoil that flails about.

Second, the team needs to know that the leader is taking action to address the situation. This is a dimension of appropriate decisiveness — a critical element of effective leadership in a complex and fluid context such as healthcare.

Third, specifics must not be explained. Those specifics — whether they involve you as the physician leader coaching the target physician, pursuing outside coaching, mandating training programs for the target physician, or disciplinary procedures — should not be shared. If leaders have questions regarding the appropriateness or legality of what should be shared, checking with your direct leader and the human resources department is prudent and recommended. Being transparent about awareness of the situation and that actions are being pursued while being guardedly vague about specifics is sound practice.

Northwestern University dispute resolution expert Leigh Thompson notes that this may be a good opportunity for getting the team training in how to engage in positive conflict encounters, thereby eschewing extreme tendencies to be either overly polite or overly critical.[164] It also can thwart the normal tendency of team members to avoid, as much as possible, problematic colleagues. As we know, in a healthcare system, such avoidance can lead to undesirable outcomes.

Here, leaders must move judiciously. We certainly do not want team members to sense that a problematic colleague has added to their normal load of activities. Rather, this training should be positioned as an opportunity to grow as a team and emerge as a stronger and more viable unit. Indeed, this is a careful dance. The primary route for physician leaders is to project authenticity.

Ultimately, it is up to the target physician to rebuild trust and demonstrate their value to the team, not only in patient care but also in relationships with team members. Of course, the physician leader has a critical role in enabling the target physician's development.

SUMMARY CHECKLIST

Specific to the target physician, the leader can also make requests of the team, including:

- **Encouragement**: The team can offer words of encouragement and positive reinforcement when they see evidence of positive changes.
- **Open Communication**: The target physician should feel comfortable discussing any challenges he may still encounter, and these should be met with understanding and, over time, a willingness to help.

- **Peer Support and Mentorship**: Pairing the target physician with a mentor or a peer within the team can provide them with additional guidance and support. This individual can serve as a trusted confidant whom the target physician can turn to for advice or assistance when navigating challenging situations.
- **Feedback and Accountability**: Constructive feedback is essential for ongoing growth and improvement. The team should continue to provide the target physician with feedback on his interactions and behaviors, highlighting areas of improvement while also acknowledging his progress. Establishing a system of mutual accountability within the team can ensure that everyone is committed to supporting each other's well-being and professional development.

CHAPTER 10

When Is It Finally Enough?

···

THREE YEARS AFTER BEING HIRED to lead the oncology service line, Kiara was a champion for the physicians in her unit. While emphasizing high standards, she showed sensitivity to the unique characteristics of those on her clinical team. She reached out to us on multiple occasions — usually to enhance the leadership and interpersonal skills of promising young physicians. Under Kiara's steady guidance, the service line made positive strides, and her team experienced growth and improved morale. Within this context, we were not surprised when Kiara asked us to work with Bren.

Like so many of the target physicians we have already discussed, Bren was a good physician with specialized expertise. In addition, she arrived with a solid research record that Kiara figured would spark the research of the unit as Bren collaborated with her colleagues.

After nearly two years, Bren never quite fit in with the team. Additionally, her curt tell-it-like-it-is style rankled nearly all her physician colleagues. Most refused to work with her on research projects — projects that Bren turned into stressful and contentious ventures. Through her interactions, Bren made it clear verbally and non-verbally that she was the smartest person in the room.

To her credit, Kiara met regularly with Bren. In most cases, Bren bristled at Kiara's efforts, gave perfunctory agreement, dismissed the seriousness of her situation, and made little progress or changes in her behavior. Disciplinary actions followed, prompting a few short-term improvements followed by rapid regression to her old habits.

Now, Kiara reached out to us, hoping that our outside coaching might help Bren enact some needed behavioral changes. Granted wide latitude, we recognized that we were one piece (perhaps a final piece) in Kiara's efforts to help Bren and salvage her career with the unit.

We met with Bren for about two months. She was defensive but polite and respectful. We discussed and practiced some interpersonal shifts — relatively minor changes. As we reviewed her progress in each meeting, she continued to focus on others' problems rather than her own.

During our final check-in with Kiara, there was no discussion of the particulars of our interactions with Bren, which was consistent with our promised confidentiality. However, we all knew that appropriate and needed behavioral changes had not occurred.

Kiara thanked us for our work with Bren and reminded us of how much she appreciated our work with others in her unit. However, Kiara was adamant, "After nearly a year of trying to help her change, I must face the fact that it's not getting better with Bren and the team. It's best to move on." When Kiara signaled to Bren that her upcoming contract would not be renewed, Bren decided to voluntarily leave, landing a promising position in another part of the country.

Even as a seasoned leader, Kiara shared her sense of frustration and disappointment. She had lost a talented clinician and lead researcher. From Kiara's perspective, her ongoing efforts at remediation — efforts that consumed time, energy, and resources — had fundamentally failed. Intellectually, Kiara knew she was making the proper decision. However, from an emotional perspective, Kiara was struggling to get her arms around what had been a period of tension.

A LACK OF SUCCESS IS NOT A FAILURE

We are not attempting to dismiss the intensity of the situation, nor are we extending a positive motivational pitch. As we discussed with Kiara, she had not failed. In fact, as a conscientious leader, she had stayed close to Bren, working on a process that provided a range of opportunities for Bren to adjust. Kiara followed a logical sequence of actions; unfortunately, Bren simply refused to take corrective actions.

Further, Kiara eschewed the easy route of tolerance. While she led Bren toward self-discovery, Bren refused to participate. No meaningful change is likely to occur unless the target physician recognizes the gap between where they are and what the unit needs. Further, even when such an awareness is present, change demands that the target physician commits to the hard work necessary for reentry and readjustment. From all indicators, Bren missed the mark on both themes.

There is an additional dimension. Although the physician and clinical team were probably unaware of all the attempts Kiara had made, they knew that she was trying to help Bren. Even more importantly, they appreciated the work Kiara had done, and they recognized that her final decision was made in the long-run best interests of the team and its overall mission. These are all wins.

Here, the classic work of social judgment theory offers an important perspective.[165] Sometimes, the gap between where the target physician is currently positioned (values and actions) and the needed expectations of the unit is simply too large to be bridged. One could argue that the existence of such gaps demonstrates a flaw in the recruiting, interviewing, and selection process.

Indeed, there may be some logic to such a claim. However, in a world where the supply of needed physician talent (especially within certain specialty areas) and growing demand for services is readily apparent, selection teams may have few options. Also, as we all know, the interviewing process is laden with biases and misreads.[166] Almost any physician can put on their game face and project a positive image during the limited range of the interviewing period.

Hopefully, from a developmental point of view, Kiara and the team have learned that a more thorough and on-point interviewing and selection process would be prudent going ahead. Bren was never appropriately socialized into the team. Committing to paying careful attention to the values and sense of fit with future candidates is wise.[167]

THE GAME HAS CHANGED

Despite our hopes, intentions, and efforts, there is a point of finality. In this regard, we are, at times, presented with an unfortunate comment and question: "We've tried everything. When is it finally enough?"

We noted earlier that physicians displaying chronic, unacceptable disruptive behaviors comprise a very small segment of the physician base — a figure usually estimated to be no higher than 5% of all physicians.[134] We have argued that within that small group, an even smaller percentage fail to respond to helpful efforts, and their behavior largely has not changed in an appreciable and acceptable manner. Our readings, discussions, and ongoing work suggest that about 20% to 30% of those in the disruptive zone will not be re-centered and rehabilitated. So, what do we do?

There is a hard reality, a consistent life lesson: *We cannot save everyone.* The decision of finality is never taken with a cavalier spirit. Further, it is not a decision of concession. Rather, it is a well-thought-through conclusion that all remediation efforts have failed to move the behavioral needle enough.

Physician leaders should keep four factors in mind. First, be sure that the patterns of remediation outlined in this book have been followed. Second, be sure that sufficient time and coaching have been provided to logically expect change from the target physician. Third, be sure that increasing consequences have been imposed. Fourth, be sure that the target physician has been well-informed and aware of consequences and how they will be imposed. A final fateful decision should never come as a shock to the target physician if discussions have been open and clear expectations have been emphasized.

The final decision that we have done all we can is a decision to move on in the best interests of your unit and your people. Usually, it is born of dual thinking. On one hand, you cannot afford to expend more time, energy, and resources on this particular target physician. On the other hand, the target physician's behaviors continue to contaminate the work spirit and culture. The stress levels on staff remain unacceptable, and the feelings of inequity and unfairness continue to build. Here, physician leaders must be willing to throw up their hands and say, "Enough!"

Let's consider an example. When Noreen was hired as department chair of neurology, she knew the two most critical and immediate expectations: (1) help the service line rise in prominence and (2) change the internal culture that seemed dominated by toxic distrust.

Knowing that her task had to be approached sequentially, Noreen launched a couple of new initiatives. One of these was to personally get involved, working with two physicians who were disrupting the team. Of the two, Anika was the most problematic physician by far.

Noreen did her research. She talked with the staff, examined the formal records (which included a litany of grievances over the past two years), and had informal meetings with Anika. Noreen was clear with Anika about expectations and why these expectations were important, and she helped Anika craft a plan of action.

Interestingly, Noreen noted that even with the plan of action in place, she did not sense that Anika was ready to accept personal responsibility. They discussed this feeling, as well as Anika's unparalleled capacity to point the finger of blame toward others after each disruptive incident. Consistent with what we have already outlined, Noreen encouraged Anika to focus on what "she could do rather than on what others should do."

As a step in the process, Noreen engaged outside coaches to work with Anika for a series of sessions — sessions that could be renewed if progress occurred.

However, there was no dramatic turnaround, no laudable success. Anika missed a number of meetings with her coach. When they did meet, Anika approached the coach with the same attitude of denial and obfuscation that she had used with Noreen. Anika remained defiant and inflexible, arguing that she must demand that her colleagues use the proper procedures (her preferred procedures). Noreen imposed a couple of intermediary disciplinary actions, which included a brief leave of absence, which was part of a progressive remedial process that had taken place over several months.

Finally, Noreen decided to sever the relationship, and she informed Anika that Anika's contract, which expired in a few months, would not be renewed. "The final unfortunate outcome," as Noreen shared.

Here is the tough part. Noreen, a driven, high-achieving, and caring leader, felt as though she had failed. Although her emotions were understandable, we disagreed. Noreen had engaged in an impressive array of actions, all designed to help Anika, all aimed at avoiding the final act of non-renewal.

We tried to help Noreen gain perspective on her actions and on the ultimate decision. We argued that successful leaders do not terminate others; rather, others, by virtue of their actions or failures to act, terminate themselves by placing the leader in an untenable position.

Again, we turn to theory. Sometimes, there is simply not a good fit between the person (and their personality and needs) and those of the unit in question.[168,169] Anika swore that she had not experienced issues during her education, residency, or in her first job at another hospital in another region of the country. Noreen understood this perspective and even used the argument when having the non-renewal conversation with Anika.

Before leaving this subject, a caveat is in order. Human resource experts urge caution with the "fit" argument as the "poor fit" justification has been used to exclude certain individuals and groups. Therefore, be certain that the lack of fit reasoning rises above any systemic or personal biases. Further, given the shortage of physician talent, the fit argument takes on a last-resort frame of thinking.

However, in the situation between Noreen and Anika, all options had been exhausted. The lack of fit disrupted the morale and intensity of the staff. The final decision was unequivocally necessary.

Most of us dread difficult or problematic performance reviews. Emotions are likely to flair, and leaders are vulnerable to being thrown off track. Similarly, the decisive meeting with a target physician is stressful for all parties.

The meeting should be carefully planned with upfront clarity regarding what to say and what not to say.

Keep in mind that this is not the time to explore creative options for remediation. That period has passed. Once a final decision has been made, one should move decisively. Hopefully, the leader has a solid line of documentation, and discussions with upper management have taken place. The issue remaining is how to deliver the final message.

The tone and content of the message is key. It is important to be direct, focusing on documentation and evidence. It is also important to be brief. While a number of "how to" sources are available, check with human resources for appropriate guidance, especially guidance particular to your unique situation — including legal guidance — before proceeding.[170]

AND ONCE AGAIN … THE REST OF THE TEAM

When a decision is made regarding severing ties with a target physician, a major part of the leader's responsibility is to address the rest of the team, explaining what they can and focusing team efforts and motivations on the tasks ahead. Here, the leader must thread a needle. Fortunately, excellent sources offer helpful suggestions, and we draw liberally from these and other research and writing.[171,172,173]

Leaders always perform under a bit of a microscope. Yet, the magnifying intensity of your team is likely ramped up during this period of change and transition. As such, we provide four guidelines to help physician leaders understand and appropriately reach out to the rest of the team.

First, you must *communicate with the team.* At times, leaders shy away from this challenge, largely because of confusion regarding what to say and fear about saying the wrong thing. Both concerns are sound and certainly understandable.

If possible, arrange a short meeting with the team as soon as possible after the target physician's decision. In this way, you can control the narrative and at least partially blunt rumors that will likely arise.

In communicating, it is important to be clear but discrete, focusing on the ultimate decision. For example, you may simply assert, "After careful consideration, a decision has been made. Beginning in January, Dr. Smith will no longer be part of our practice." Avoid saying too much more about the decision, recognizing that it is unwise and risky to divulge details.

The rest of the team is certainly cognizant of some of what has been going on regarding the target physician, and they should appreciate that you cannot and will not address issues that should be held between you and the target physician. If queried, it is appropriate to assert the obvious. "As you all know, I cannot address specifics here."

Second, *respect the target physician.* By this, we mean that leaders must shun the somewhat natural tendency to demonize the person who has been a disruptive and stressful source for many on the team. In addition, be clear that respect toward the target physician is expected during their remaining tenure.

Here, the leader must model the desired actions. For example, "Dr. Smith has solid clinical skills. I'm hopeful that he will be happier in another organization. It is my intention to respond respectfully toward Dr. Smith as he completes his stay with us and serves our patients during this time of transition." Here, the leader signals respect and encourages the focus to be directed toward positive patient outcomes.

Third is a factor that is both critically important and frequently missed. Leaders, as best as they can, must *explain what the decision and departure of the target physician mean for the rest of the team.* For example, "We will be recruiting to fill Dr. Smith's position, and I will be asking several of you to help in this regard."

Point out the negative impacts that may befall the team, as well as efforts being considered or undertaken to mitigate those effects. "We will have to adjust to serve Dr. Smith's patients. I will talk with each of you regarding how best to handle the patient load. In addition, each of us, including me, will have to accept additional call. I have already met with leadership about some ideas regarding call coverage. I encourage you to share ideas with me." Note that this action-oriented piece of the conversation may need to be repeated in a follow-up meeting.

The target physician likely had relationships that would change, and the remaining physicians may be alerted to their own disruptive behavior that needs attention. All of this can create an emotional response that inhibits engaging in action, at least at the outset.

Two key themes arise here. On one hand, the leader is making no effort to sugarcoat the reality everyone is facing. At the same time, the leader is engaging the team to accept ownership for finding solutions that work to the benefit of all. One should not expect that the team will be happy with the additional demands that may be placed on them. There is no need to argue. Rather, leaders should project that the team must move forward to enhance its mission.

Fourth, leaders should be open to *asking for and addressing questions from the team.* As a leader, it is important to project the attitude that the team is planning *together on* how to move ahead. It's subtle, but planning with the team starts with the leader. Further, the leader takes on an inordinate degree of responsibility for how progress is structured. Listen; incorporate ideas from the team, but accept that the bulk of the heavy lifting comes from the physician leader.

LESSONS OF LEADERSHIP

We worked with Erica for several months as she grappled with Tom, a target physician whose aggressive and belligerent approach seemed to be a constant source of frustration for Erica and the team. We walked through successive approaches as Erica established boundaries, clarified expectations, and worked to help Tom become a steadier and more collaborative colleague. Her frustrations were evident, and with classic understatement, she shared, "My leader role would not be bad if it weren't for Tom. I had no idea I'd inherit a problem as consuming as he has been."

We acknowledged Erica's feelings but pushed further. We affirmed that Tom's was a particularly tough case — perhaps an extreme case. We also encouraged some perspective-taking. No leadership role is ever void of pesky people issues. While Tom may be an outlier, we suggested to Erica that she would encounter other pressing and demanding individuals and situations as her leadership career progressed.

We also reminded her that she was learning and growing in her leadership role due, in no small part, to the behaviors she had adopted to address matters with Tom. While we never seek them, leadership is often forged and refined in the cauldron of adversities. If nothing more, we were suggesting to Erica that her mindset toward Tom could be one of both stopping undesirable actions and developing leadership capacities that yield an expanded range of leadership skills.

Finally, we offer leaders a statement of reality that affects a small percentage of target physicians: When all practical options have been enacted and escalating repercussions have been exhausted, recognize that there are situations in which target physicians cannot be successfully redirected. In short, even the most adept leaders cannot save everyone.

SUMMARY CHECKLIST

This chapter addresses the reality of moving along from our expressed desire and efforts to salvage the tenure of a target physician. A few important practical themes arise:

- Physician leaders should consider the valuable interpersonal and leadership lessons that have been learned by working with the target physician. These learnings may help the leader (as well as others) better assimilate future physicians into the team.
- Leaders should always project respect toward target physicians, even at this final juncture.
- Perspective is important. Remember that it is not the actions of physician leaders that have led to the termination decision. Rather, target physicians (through actions and inactions) are responsible for the ultimate decision.
- Physician leaders must pay special attention to the rest of the team during this time of change and transition. Communication and touch points are vital for the clinical team.

CHAPTER 11

Conclusions

....

W HILE WE DON'T RECOMMEND EXTERNAL COACHING as an immediate response to the behavior of your target physicians, coaching can certainly be helpful in supporting *you*. As we've outlined in this book, we recommend taking a progressive approach: addressing concerns, performance issues, missed expectations, and consequences in service of fostering the development of target physicians and facilitating their reintegration into the team. We have encouraged you, as physician leaders, to work diligently to salvage talent and refocus the unit toward a more positive culture.

We began with a description of your target physician, sometimes called a "distressed physician," even though the circumstances surrounding the disruptive behavior are much more complex than the distress that comes with the vagaries of life. Physicians engaging in disruptive behavior negatively affect patient care, interpersonal relationships, and team dynamics, all while derailing their own careers.

We encouraged early intervention, and we outlined an approach for engaging with the target physician to encourage their development, hold them accountable, and strengthen relationships with the team. We addressed the inevitable question of "When is it enough?" and acknowledged the emotional aspects of this dimension of your leadership role.

In this concluding chapter of the book, we aim to coach you once last time, drawing upon the unique challenges that our clients and audiences raise when it comes to dealing with disruptive behavior on your team. We outline five nuances that require more guidance than the frameworks and checklists in the previous chapters. In nearly all cases, there is an emotional component to these themes, and we highly recommend talking with a mentor or colleague as you move through them.

Unlike previous chapters, you may not be able to see the particulars of your experience in these examples. But you will see an echo of our approach throughout the book: seek to understand through conversation that aims to build trust and a sense of partnership in resolving the issue at hand; proceed with caution, clarity, and confidence; and intervene in ways that align with your values alongside those of your team and organization.

119

WHAT IF THE TARGET PHYSICIAN IS A FRIEND?

This may be one of the more emotionally charged challenges for physician leaders. Since many physician leaders attain their roles through internal promotions, it is likely that they have already established a range of relationships with the physicians they are now called to lead. Consistent with experience, leadership theory underscores that physician leaders have closer, more trusting, and more open relations with some members of the team than they do with others.[174]

Further, the leader's willingness to interact and communicate also varies as interpersonal connections mesh more smoothly with some than with others.[174] Within this context, it is likely that some peers are friends — friends who now interact with leaders in new and different roles.

Unfortunately, the plot thickens when friends emerge as target physicians whose disruptive actions must be addressed. In some cases, disruptions can be *more* likely if target physicians feel as though they have a strong and understanding relationship with the physician leader. Complex and stressful, such actions are part of the leader's responsibilities.

We begin with a theoretical consideration that is more easily stated than enacted. As noted above, leaders (like all of us) are emotional beings who naturally feel closer to some people than to others. For this very reason, leaders should maintain a degree of *social distance* between themselves and those being led.

Theory suggests that distance (social and psychological) allows leaders to maintain objectivity and enact difficult decisions based on organizational and clinical needs rather than emotional and social factors.[175,176] For these reasons, physician leaders must distinguish between personal connections and workplace demands — a process that may feel awkward in situations where the parties have been close and friendships have developed.

The preferred approach to such matters is to *clarify the situation* and establish the *needs and expectations* that must be achieved. This is best done early and repeated periodically, as necessary. It's reasonable to acknowledge friendships and still underscore that objective, whole-system decisions will be necessary — decisions that emphasize work-related issues. These are decisions where organizational needs supersede friendships.

Fortunately, most people understand and appreciate the reality that a friend hat and a leader hat cannot always be worn together. Yet, this awareness does not diminish the emotional impact that ensuing discussions will spark for our target physicians.

Here, we are often asked whether having direct, improvement-focused discussions (along with escalating consequences) will lead to a fracturing of the relationship and friendship between the physician leader and the target physician. The short answer is that the relationship will likely be affected — a reality most of us understand but wish to avoid. Logically, the target physician may become more tenuous and less revealing with their leader than was previously the case.

Further, drawing the distinction between personal and work relationships is a difficult and fragile line. Here, target physicians may play the friendship card. Physician leaders must be unequivocal, asserting that they value the friendship of the target physician while drawing a distinction regarding what is best for the overall team. Once again, the effort to distinguish personal feelings from business and clinical needs is critical.

The larger issue here is perceived equity and fairness within the team.[177] If others believe that a target physician is receiving special or preferential treatment because of their friendship with the leader, perceptions of team equity are violated, and the leader's credibility will be undermined or even derailed. Linda Hill and Kent Lineback punch this theme home with distinct clarity: "If you're reluctant to discipline someone because of the harm it might do to your relationships, then your ties to that person will prevent you from doing your job as the boss."[178]

Let's consider an example — one of the more revealing and unfortunate episodes we have encountered. Approaching mid-career, Jason was drawn to leave his employer and assume the role of chief executive officer of a growing marketing firm with national clients. His decision was complex and affected by a variety of factors. However, as Jason openly shared, one key consideration was the opportunity to work with Roy, an admired colleague who coincidentally had been Jason's college roommate and remained his best friend. In some regards, the opportunity to work with an admired and trusted friend "sealed the deal" for Jason.

Within the first four months, Jason was able to isolate systemic problems within his new team — many of which involved or revolved around Roy. Jason struggled and lamented and, understandably, looked for every option to avoid confronting Roy. However, realizing the broader stakes at hand, he knew that a developmental conversation was inevitable.

Jason talked with Roy, shared concerns, and carefully outlined the actions and interpersonal changes that seemed essential. Jason listened. He took time. He vowed to help. He offered sensitivity while focusing on a clear need for change. In short, despite considerable levels of discomfort, Jason did what he needed to do as the CEO. He presented expectations, needs, and developmental options.

As one might expect, everything did not progress smoothly. Soon, Jason was forced to make the hard decision to remove Roy from his leadership role — a role that focused on a major client. Seeing the inevitable playing out, Roy resigned. Client concerns ebbed, and most internal managers recognized that with Roy out of the equation, workflow and morale improved markedly.

Discussing these matters with Jason, we posed a naïve question: "Is Roy still one of your best friends?" Jason did not waver as he expressed one of the unfortunate truisms of leadership: "Roy hasn't spoken to me for the last three years."

While you are likely already in a leadership role, this is one of the things we counsel those considering stepping into one. There is much to gain but also some necessary and painful losses. At this point, we encourage you to acknowledge the potential of loss as you move forward to effectively execute your leadership responsibilities.

WHAT IF THE TARGET PHYSICIAN IS A DISRUPTIVE BOSS?

During a recent workshop's question-and-answer session, we were asked, "What do we do when the target physician is a superior?" Although they may lack direct formal authority, physician leaders may still have some influence. Let's explore a few key themes.

We begin by encouraging caution and control. Some superiors want and are responsive to constructive feedback. Others, even when expressing the desire for helpful input, display behaviors suggesting that expressions of openness are neither appreciated nor accepted. Attempts to help can be viewed as criticisms, which may be interpreted as signaling a lack of loyalty.

Accordingly, we begin by encouraging physician leaders to understand the territory, carefully read their superiors, and be judicious when offering feedback — even essential and constructive feedback. In short, while some superiors claim they want to know how they can improve, their egos are too fragile to handle criticism. Accordingly, rule number one is to move carefully and judiciously. If one is unsure whether to offer constructive feedback, it's generally best to hold back until you sense an appropriate and receptive opening.

Research suggests the importance of trying to understand the pressures and challenges that the boss confronts.[179] Further, it's helpful to view the boss as an emotional being, awash with ego and insecurities like all of us.[180] Despite a strong and objective veneer, defensiveness should be expected. An example may be helpful.

Layne is a physician leader who has the respect of most of the physicians in her hospital system. After a recent restructuring, few were surprised when Layne was named CMO of the growing hospital system. Peers felt that her new role and responsibilities were well-earned and deserved.

Assuming her duties, Layne recognized that her new boss, Jackson, was problematic, even though Jackson served in the C-suite as the highest-ranking physician in the system. What, if anything, should Layne do? Having ascertained Jackson's openness and readiness for "constructive feedback," how can Layne prepare for a discussion with Jackson?

Messaging becomes important. We advise *framing feedback* in terms that speak to superiors and their unique needs. Superiors generally think in terms of metrics, focusing on outcomes that affect patient satisfaction, increased revenue, decreased costs, and the capacity to position the unit for ongoing success. They prefer to deal with facts over vague impressions and feelings.

In our example, Layne wants to make Jackson aware that the nursing staff desires more attention, support, and recognition from Jackson. Here, Layne could simply encourage Jackson to offer occasional affirmations when seeing nurses. Or Layne could explain that she is concerned about potential nurse turnover, which has escalated recently.

Further, she may share data obtained through exit interviews, which points to a correlation between turnover and a lack of appreciation and sense of contribution that nurses receive, a concern prompted by exit comments that "top leadership could care less about us."

The latter approach further locks in on Jackson's oft-phrased concern about staffing and losing talented clinicians and nursing staff to rivals. Accordingly, if nothing else, Jackson's attention to the matter has likely been piqued.

When approaching disruptive superiors, physician leaders should offer input and perspective rather than demands for action. Again, messaging is key. Further, like so many themes throughout this book, we suggest a process of engagement — in this case, a process comprised of four steps.

First, physician leaders should begin with *intent and affirmation*, emphasizing their commitment to the organization and underscoring their desire and commitment for positive working relationships with the target superior. Here, it is helpful to note the superior's positive qualities.

Second, physician leaders should *request permission* to share personal thoughts and perspectives that may be useful and helpful. Additionally, if appropriate, physician leaders should share the ways in which they have grappled with the same issue that they plan to address.

Third, *deliver the message.* Here, we encourage sensitivity. Even though superiors may espouse their capacity for brutal honesty, there is little to gain from such an approach. Instead, we favor *sensitive honesty* — moving carefully and consistently evaluating the superior's level of emotional acceptance. Importantly, this is no place for winging the message. Think it through, anticipate how the superior is likely to respond, and play out contingencies and options if matters begin to veer off the rails.

Fourth and finally, *thank and reaffirm,* emphasizing your appreciation for being able to share your thoughts and again sharing your intent to work with the superior for the best outcomes for the unit. We will not be trite. These interactions are potentially explosive and must be approached with appropriate deference.

HOW CAN I ASSERT MYSELF AND HAVE RESPECTFUL DISAGREEMENTS?

The following question initially was unexpected. It came from a trio of younger physicians early in their leadership roles. Maya expressed the need directly, as others in our workshop nodded in affirmation. "I have a strong need to behave respectfully and cooperatively. How can I be firm, appropriately represent my ideas, assert the behavioral changes needed, and not be seen as behaving disrespectfully?"

There are some important antecedents to this query. Physician leaders come by this concern honestly; often, their training involves a clear hierarchy and deference to attending physicians and teaching faculty. The question itself portrays a physician with both sensitivity and self-awareness, one who did not absorb the one-way communication tropes that medical education is known for.

The question also probably comes from experience with assertive colleagues who are willing to throw their weight around to push their points, demanding attention and action. In some ways, these colleagues are admired for their ability to drive their interests and concerns. Yet, there is a deep reluctance and a need to avoid what can devolve into an overly aggressive and even bullying posture.

Here, the physician is clear about what is sought and what is to be avoided. Digging a bit further, she is concerned about how to advocate for herself in the presence of a target physician, likely to respond defensively and aggressively.

It is important to recognize that directness, firmness, and advocacy of a point of view need not be inconsistent with interpersonal sensitivity and respect. Like so many things, the key is in one's approach and style of communication. Further, we laud bright and talented people who can refrain from swaying their character by modeling others' aggressive approaches. With all that in mind, here is a straightforward five-step process for you to consider.[14]

First, *listen carefully to the arguments that others are presenting.* Try to be crystal clear regarding what they are advocating. We talked about listening earlier in the book; remember to put your interests on hold and truly concentrate on what the other party is saying. Center not only on the details being expressed but also look for the emotions and needs behind the words. If you are uncertain, then check. For example, state, "If I'm hearing you correctly, you feel you work harder than most people in the practice. Is that right?"

The point here is to listen and acknowledge that you have heard their message. There is no need to argue the merits of what they feel. In fact, except where there are clear facts, it's an impossible slog to attempt to discount impressions.

Second, *show affirmation* — a verification of the target physician's feelings and beliefs. "When you feel that you work harder than others, it's frustrating, and I recognize that those feelings are magnified when you are called out or reported by those same colleagues. Is that right?"

Note that statements of affirmation are not statements of agreement. Rather, the leader is signaling understanding and empathy —important factors for an ongoing developmental relationship between the physician leader and the target physician.

The third step is to *express the need and reasoning behind the need.* As one moves to expression and reasoning, the leader must clearly state the actions and outcomes that are essential, usually achieved by focusing on the overall needs of the practice or unit of concern. Further, as we have discussed in earlier chapters, leaders must carefully delineate *why* the desired needs are essential.[130]

The fourth step is to *check for understanding*. We all know that one of the major barriers to effective communication comes from parties hearing and focusing on differing messages. Therefore, a perception check is warranted. Be straightforward, "Do you understand what we need here and why it is so important?" Hopefully, the response extends beyond a simple affirmative "yes," where the target physician can express what they have heard and interpreted in their own words.

The fifth step is to *be pragmatic*. Realistically, the entire process we have just described may need to be repeated. Here, subsequent iterations of the process will drive home the issues and needs while maintaining respect.

HOW DO I NAVIGATE THE "WHY ME?" QUESTION?

"Why me?" It may be the most common question we hear as we work with target physicians, and you may hear it as you address disruptive behavior. Although it comes in various forms, the target physician is typically expressing resentment for being singled out. One target physician with whom we worked spoke bluntly about the issue: "This coaching only works if you're meeting with everyone. I'm not the only one responsible for the conditions and the situation we are addressing." While the commentary may be reasonable and even accurate, what emerges is a form of deflection that seeks to shift or broaden the realm of responsibility.

As we discussed in Chapter 3, disruptive behavior is a complex behavioral display that is likely sparked by several interrelated dynamics and pressures. Here, we encourage physician leaders to center their responses on the target physician. Remind the target physician that your focus is on them since their own behavior is the only behavior that they can truly change.

It is best to avoid drawing others into the immediate conversation — discussing others serves no need, and any attempt is likely to intensify the target physician's perceptions of unfair treatment.

Generally, we do not allow the conversation to digress and prefer straightforward statements such as, "I understand how you feel. However, let's focus on you and how you can respond to these situations." The acknowledgment is important, as it indicates that you are not dismissing the target physician's feelings. This approach should be followed by a timely pivot to what the target physician can do.

On occasion, target physicians refuse to be involved in coaching unless others are receiving the same attention. Again, we offer direct statements such as, "I hope we can continue to work together. It's important. But ultimately, it's your decision." In this manner, we place responsibility squarely back on the target physician.

It is likely that these exchanges will result in awkward silence and open displays of frustration and disappointment from the target physician. Here, physician leaders must continue the process of remediation and fight the temptation to justify themselves and the rest of the staff.

HOW DO I STEM THE TIDE OF NEGATIVITY?

During the question-and-answer phase of a recent presentation to an audience of emerging physician leaders, the query was posed. "You've made the case against the destructive force of negative labels. What do we do, as leaders, when the negativity is already ingrained within the team?"

Here, we draw from our knowledge of decision paradigms and decision-making biases.[181] At some point, it is likely that the target physician's behavior is being viewed through the prism of past behaviors and the assumed meaning those actions have carried. As such, each action is placed in a preconceived perceptual context. Accordingly, a form of confirmation bias exists, leading people to see what they expect to see.[182]

This context can be especially challenging for target physicians as they attempt to make corrective actions. As such, a relatively straightforward action is woven with a thread of suspicion. "Jim just apologized" quickly becomes, "Yes, Jim apologized. But I wonder what's up his sleeve — what's really going on?" As an outsider, I find it somewhat easy to recognize that questioning Jim's motives is probably a reflection of the depth of the trust chasm that exists between parties.

The primary approach of progressive leaders is three-fold. First, the leader must demonstrate respectful behavior toward the target physician. Here, leaders must avoid the temptation to participate in negativity toward the target, refusing to engage in even subtle non-verbal behaviors. All hinges on a theme we stress in our workshops: *leaders must stay above the fray*. This is especially challenging since leaders, like the rest of the team, are likely to have strong emotional reactions to the target physician.

Second, the leader should project a *forward-thinking attitude*, emphasizing that the team must move forward to achieve its mission. While a target physician can be a stumbling block, the focus should shift from the troubles created by the target physician to how the team can move forward while the leader helps the target physician become reintegrated with the team. Rather than lament the situation and yearn for how we wish things would be, leaders must focus on "how do we make this work given the issues with which we must work."[183]

Third, the leader can help the team look for ways to include rather than exclude the target physician. Leaders must blunt the natural tendency to have as little contact as possible with the target physician. Team members are unlikely to have a positive shift in attitude toward the target member without touchpoints where progress (even small progress) can be displayed and experienced.

A FINAL PERSPECTIVE

As noted in the title, this book is intended as a guide — a guide to help physician leaders address one of the most problematic interpersonal issues they are likely to face. Yet, our work is only a guide. Each physician leader must adapt their approach given the unique parameters within which they work. It is our hope that this book offers help in this important undertaking.

SUMMARY CHECKLIST

This chapter has offered practical solutions in response to questions we have received about specific circumstances. In doing so, we hope we've given you the confidence to address disruptive behavior with the tools and frameworks provided and the deep understanding that allows you to tackle any version of these circumstances when they come your way.

The checklists at the end of each chapter have been written as a summary for you to return to periodically as your impact as a physician leader deepens and expands. With that in mind, some broad points seem appropriate for this final checklist summary.

- Use the five-step process of respect, which emphasizes (1) listening to the target physicians, (2) providing affirmations, (3) expressing your needs with attendant reasoning and logic, (4) checking with the other party to ensure understanding, and (5) progressing through successive iterations of the process as needed.
- Keep the focus on the target physician, resisting challenges to the behaviors of colleagues and staff.
- Establish appropriate social distance to differentiate personal friendships from workplace needs, expectations, and demands.

- When addressing disruptive superiors, move judiciously and focus on messaging by using the four-step process of intent and affirmation, requesting permission to provide feedback, clearly delivering the message, and offering thanks and reaffirmation.
- When dealing with superiors, be sure to emphasize that your concern is twofold: ensuring appropriate unit outcomes and signaling your support for the superior.
- Recognize that direct expressions of unequivocal needs and behavioral outcomes can be achieved while maintaining sensitivity and respect.

REFERENCES

1. Paramo JC, Welsh DJ, Kirby J, et al. *2018 ACS Governors Survey: The Disruptive and Impaired Surgeon.* American College of Surgeons Bulletin. May 1, 2019. https://www.facs.org/for-medical-professionals/news-publications/news-and-articles/bulletin/2019/06/2018-acs-governors-survey-burnout-a-growing-challenge/.

2. American Medical Association. AMA Code of Medical Ethics. 2017. https://code-medical-ethics.ama-assn.org.

3. Kegan R, Lahey L. Adult Development and Organizational Leadership. In: Nohira N, Khutrana R, eds. *Handbook of Leadership Theory and Practice.* Boston: Harvard Business Press; 2010:770.

4. Burchell M, Robin J. *The Great Workplace: How to Build It, How to Keep It, and Why It Matters.* San Francisco: Jossey-Bass; 2011.

5. Nemecek, P. The Decision Bridge: A Model for Coaching Distressed Physicians. *International Journal of Evidenced Based Coaching and Mentoring.* 2023;17:108-121.

6. Shanafelt TD. Suicidal Ideation and Attitudes Regarding Help Seeking in U.S. Physicians Relative to the U.S. Working Population. *Mayo Clin Proc.* 2021;96(8):2067–2080. https://doi.org/10.1016/j.mayocp.2021.01.033.

7. Medscape. *Physician Burnout & Depression Report 2022: Stress, Anxiety, and Anger.* Medscape. 2022. www.medscape.com/slideshow/2022-lifestyle-burnout-6014664?icd=login_success_email_match_norm#1.

8. American College of Healthcare Executives. Top Issues Confronting Hospitals in 2021. 2022. https://www.ache.org/learning-center/research/about-the-field/top-issues-confronting-hospitals.

9. Association of American Medical Colleges. *The Complexities of Physician Supply and Demand from 2019 to 2034.* Washington, DC: AAMC;2021.

10. Hoff T, Trovato K. Burnout Among Family Physicians in the United States: A Review of the Literature. *Qual Manag in Health Care.* 2024:33(1):1–11. https://doi.org/10.1097/QMH.0000000000000439.

11. Payerchin R. Physician Roundtable: Burnout Continues to Escalate. *Medical Economics.* 2022; 99(1).

12. Skeff KM, Brown-Johnson CG, Ash SM, Winget M, Kerem Y. Professional Behavior and Value Erosion: A Qualitative Study of Physicians and the Electronic Health Record. *J Healthc Manag.* 2022;67(5):339 -352. https://doi.org/10.1097/JHM-D-21-00070.

13. Kusy M. Six intentional Ways To Build Teams of Everyday Civility (and Proactively Erode Toxic Behaviors). *Physician Leadership Journal.* 2020;7(5):65–70.

14. Stoner CR, Stoner JS. *Inspired Physician Leadership: Creating Influence and Impact* (2nd ed.). Washington DC: American Association for Physician Leadership;2023.

15. Bennis W. *Managing People Is Like Herding Cats: Warren Bennis on Leadership.* Provo UT: Executive Excellence Publishing;1997.

16. Stoner CR, Gilligan JF. *The Adversity Challenge: How Successful Leaders Bounce Back from Setbacks.* Provo UT: Executive Excellence Publishing;2006.

17. Burns DJ, Mooney D. Transcollegial Leadership: A New Paradigm for Leadership. *International Journal of Educational Management*. 2018;32(1):57–70. https://doi.org/10.1108/IJEM-05-2016-0114.

18. American Medical Association. Physicians with Disruptive Behavior. 2017. AMA Code of Medical Ethics. 2017. https://code-medical-ethics.ama-assn.org?ethics-opinions/physicians-disruptive-behavior.

19. Holmes J, Olson L. Dealing with Disruptive Physicians. Medical Group Management Association. 2016. https://www.mgma.com/articles/dealing-with-disruptive-physicians.

20. Noyes AL. Navigating the Hierarchy: Communicating Power Relationships in Collaborative Health Care Groups. *Management Communication Quarterly*. 2022;36(1):62–91. https://doi.org/10.1177/08933189211025737.

21. Van Norman GA. Abusive and Disruptive Behavior in the Surgical Team. *AMA Journal of Ethics*. 2015;17(3):215–220. https://doi.org/10.1001/journalofethics.2015.17.3.ecas3-1503.

22. Samenow CP, Swiggart W, Spickard A. A CME Course Aimed at Addressing Disruptive Physician Behavior. *Physician Executive*. 2008;34(1):32–40.

23. Samenow CP, Worley L, Neufeld R, Fishel T, Swiggart W. Transformative Learning in a Professional Development Course Aimed at Addressing Disruptive Physician Behavior: A Composite Case Study. *Academic Medicine*. 2013;88(1):117–123. https://doi.org/10.1001/journalofethics.2015.17.3.ecas3-1503.

24. Tennessee Medical Foundation. Handling Distressed Physician Behaviors. 2016. https://e-tmf.org/app/uploads/2016/02/TMF-Distressed-Physician-Behavior2016.pdf.

25. Baumeister RF, Tierney J. *Willpower: Rediscovering the Greatest Human Strength*. New York: Penguin Books;2012.

26. Anderson CJ. The Psychology of Doing Nothing: Forms of Decision Avoidance from Reason and Emotion. *Psychological Bulletin*. 2003;129(1):139–167. https://doi.org/10.1037/0033-2909.129.1.139.

27. Morton K, Pister K. Coaching: A Useful Approach To Disruptive Behavior. *Physician Leadership Journal*. 2016;13(1), 55-57.

28. Selye H. *The Stress of Life (revised edition)*. New York: McGraw-Hill;1978.

29. Swiggert WH, Dewey CM, Hickson GB, Finlayson AJR, Spickard WA. A Plan for Identification, Treatment, and Remediation of Disruptive Behavior in Physicians. *Front Health Serv Manage*. 2009; 25(4):3–11. https://doi.org/10.1097/01974520-200904000-00002.

30. Farrington DP, Murray J. (eds.). *Labeling Theory: Empirical Tests*. New York: Routledge; 2017.

31. Rosenthal R, Jackson L. Pygmalion in the Classroom. *The Urban Review*. 1968;3(1):16–20. https://doi.org/10.1007/BF02322211.

32. Wilkinson T, Wade W. 2009. A Blueprint to Access Professionalism: Results of a Systematic Review. *Academic Medicine*. 2009;84(5):551–558. https://doi.org/10.1097/ACM.0b013e31819fbaa2.

33. Martin W, Hemphill P. *Taming Disruptive Behavior*. Tampa, FL: American College of Physician Executives; 2012.

34. Adams JS. Toward an Understanding of Inequity. *Journal of Abnormal and Social Psychology*. 1963;67:422–436. https://doi.org/10.1037/h0040968.

35. Mowday RT. Equity Theory Predictions of Behavior in Organizations. In: Steers RM, Porter LW, Bigley GA (eds.). *Motivation and Leadership at Work* (6th edition). New York: McGraw-Hill;1996.

36. Riberro N, Semedo AS, Gomes D, Bernardino R, Singh S. The Effect of Workplace Bullying on Burnout. *Management Research Review*. 2022;45(6):824-840.

37. Sidhu AK, Singh H, Sandeep SV, Kumar R. Job Stress and Its Impact on Health of Employees: A Study Among Officers and Supervisors. *The Journal of Management Development*. 2020;39(2):125–144. https://doi.org/10.1108/JMD-01-2019-0004.

38. Rossano JW, Berger S, Penny DJ. 2020. The Hard Talk: Dealing with the Disruptive Physician. *Progress in Pediatric Cardiology*. 2020;59:101315. https://doi.org/10.1016/j.ppedcard.2020.101315.

39. Caponeccha C, Wyatt A. *Preventing Workplace Bullying: An Evidenced-Based Guide for Managers and Employees*. London: Routledge;2011.

40. Chakraborti C, Boonyasai RT, Wright SM, Kern DE. A Systematic Review of Teamwork Training Interventions in Medical Student and Resident Education. *J Gen Intern Med*. 2008 Jun;23(6):846–853. https://doi.org/10.1007/s11606-008-0600-6.

41. Iqbal M. Promoting Collaborative and Teamwork Competency in Medical Students. Harvard Macy Institute Blog. April 13, 2020. https://harvardmacy.org/blog/promoting-collaborative-and-teamwork.

42. Baker DP, Salas E, King H, Battles J, Barach P. The Role of Teamwork in the Professional Education of Physicians: Current Status and Assessment Recommendations. *The Joint Commission Journal on Quality and Patient Safety*. 2005;31(4):185-202. https://doi.org/10.1016/S1553-7250(05)31025-7.

43. Maslach C, Leiter M.P. How to Measure Burnout Accurately and Ethically. *Harvard Business Review*. 2021;7.

44. Shuttengruber V, Krings F. Positive and Negative Spillover Effects: Managing Multiple Goals in Middle Adulthood. In: Spini D, Widmer E. (eds.). *Withstanding Vulnerability throughout Adult Life*. Singapore: Palgrave Macmillan;2023: 31-47. https://doi.org/10.1007/978-981-19-4567-0_3.

45. Tawfik DS, Shanafelt TD, Dyrbye LN, Sinsky CA, West CP, et al. Personal and Professional Factors Associated With Work-Life Integration Among US Physicians. *JAMA Network Open*. 2021 May 3;4(5). https://doi.org/10.1001/jamanetworkopen.2021.11575.

46. Murray E, Lo B, Pollack L, Donelan K, Catania J, et al. The Impact of Health Information on the Internet on Health Care and the Physician-patient Relationship: National US Survey Among 1.050 US physicians. J of Med Internet Res. 2003;5(3), e17. https://doi.org/10.2196/jmir.5.3.e17.

47. Dyrbye LN, Shanafelt TD, Sinsky CA, Cipriano PF, Bhatt J, et al. Burnout Among Health Care Professionals: A Call to Explore And Address This Underrecognized Threat to Safe, High-Quality Care. National Academy of Medicine Discussion Paper. July 5, 2017. https://nam.edu/burnout-among-health-care-professionals-a-call-to-explore-and-address-this-underrecognized-threat-to-safe-high-quality-care.

48. Nembhard IM, Edmondson AC. (Making It Safe: The Effects of Leader Inclusiveness and Professional Status on Psychological Safety and Improvement Efforts in Health Care Teams. *Journal of Organizational Behavior.* 2006;27(7):941–966. https://doi.org/10.1002/job.413.

49. Hill LA. Becoming the Boss. *Harvard Business Review.* 2007;85(1):48–56.

50. Gallo A. How to Manage Your Former Peers. *Harvard Business Review.* December 19, 2012. https://hbr.org/2012/12/how-to-manage-your-former-peer. https://doi.org/10.1108/IJEM-02-2022-0074.

51. Haskins ME. Leading Peers in an Academic Setting: Insights from the Front lines. *International Journal of Educational Management.* 2022;36(5):828–835.

52. Hills L. Managing a Team of Former Peers. *J Med Pract Manage.* 2016:31(6):274–379.

53. Uhl-Bien M. Relationship-based Approach to Leadership: Development of Leader-Member Exchange (LMX) Theory of Leadership Over 25 years. *The Leadership Quarterly.* 1995;6(2):219–247. https://doi.org/10.1016/1048-9843(95)90036-5.

54. Homan AC, Gündemir S, Buengeler C, van Kleef GA. Leading Diversity: Towards a Theory of Functional Leadership in Diverse Teams. *Journal of Applied Psychology.* 2020;105(10):1101. https://doi.org/10.1037/apl0000482.

55. Cota AA, Dion KL. Salience of Gender and Sex Composition of ad hoc Groups: An Experimental Test of Distinctiveness Theory. *Journal of Personality and Social Psychology.* 1986;50(4):770–776. doi:10.1037/0022-3514.50.4.770.

56. West CP, Dyrbye LN, Shanafelt TD. Physician Burnout: Contributors, Consequences and Solutions. *J Intern Med.* 2018;283(6):516–529. https://doi.org/10.1111/joim.12752.

57. The Physicians Foundation. 2016 Survey of America's Physicians: Practice Patterns and Perspectives. The Physicians Foundation. https://physiciansfoundation.org/wp-content/uploads/2017/12/Biennial_Physician_Survey_2016.pdf.

58. Shanafelt TD, Dyrbye LN, West CP, Trockel M, Tutty M, et al. Career Plans of US Physicians After the First 2 Years of the COVID-19 Pandemic. *Mayo Clin Proc.* 2023;98(11):1629–1640. https://doi.org/10.1016/j.mayocp.2023.07.006.

59. The Physicians Foundation. 2023 Survey of America's Physicians: Practice Patterns and Perspectives. The Physicians Foundation. 2023. https://physiciansfoundation.org/wp-content/uploads/PF23_Brochure-Report_Americas-Physicians_V2b-1-2.pdf.

60. Gold KJ, Andrew LB, Goldman EB, Schwenk TL. "I would never want to have a mental health diagnosis on my record": A Survey of Female Physicians on Mental Health Diagnosis, Treatment, and Reporting. *General Hospital Psychiatry.* 2016;43:51–57. https://doi.org/10.1016/j.genhosppsych.2016.09.004.

61. Johnson B. *Polarity Management: Identifying and Managing Unsolvable Problems.* Amhurst, MA: HRD Press;1992.

62. Friedman BD, Allen KN. Systems Theory. In: Friedman BD, Allen, KN (eds.) *Essentials of Clinical Social Work.* Thousand Oaks, CA: Sage;2014:3–20. https://doi.org/10.4135/9781483398266.n2.

63. Smith-Acuna S. *Systems Theory in Action: Applications to Individuals, Couples, and Family Therapy.* Hoboken, NJ: Wiley;2010.

64. Kast FE, Rosenzweig JE. *Organization and Management: A Systems Approach.* New York: McGraw-Hill;1974.

65. Brigham TC, Barden AL, Dopp A, Hengerer J, Kaplan B, et al. A Journey to Construct an All-Encompassing Conceptual Model of Factors Affecting Clinician Well-Being and Resilience. NAM Discussion Paper. National Academy of Medicine. 2018. https://doi.org/10.31478/201801b.

66. Maslach C, Schaufeli WB, Leiter MP. Job Burnout. *Annual Review of Psychology.* 2001;52(1): 397–422. https://doi.org/10.1146/annurev.psych.52.1.397.

67. Hakim AC, Solomon M. *Working with Difficult People.* New York: TarcherPerigee;2016.

68. Sawyer RJ, Sloan A. Archetypes of Burned-out Physicians and How to Help Them. *Physician Leadership Journal.* 2022;9(5):36–39. https://doi.org/10.55834/plj.7733527450.

69. Charan R. Conquering a Culture of Indecision. *Harvard Business Review.* 2006;84(1):108–117.

70. Duckworth A. *Grit: The Power of Passion and Perseverance.* New York: Scribner;2018.

71. Atkinson JS, Feather NT. *A Theory of Achievement Motivation.* New York: John Wiley & Sons;1966.

72. McClelland DC. *The Achievement Motive.* New York: Irvington;1976.

73. Seppala E. *Why Compassion Is a Better Managerial Tactic Than Toughness.* Empathy: HBR Emotional Intelligence Series. Boston: Harvard Business Review Press;2017.

74. Hicks R, McCracken J. The Motivational Profile of an Effective Physician Leader. *Physician Executive.* 2014;40(3):102–105.

75. Morton K, Pister K. Coaching: A Useful Approach to Disruptive Behavior. *Physician Leadership Journal.* 2016;13(1):55–57.

76. Landman K. The Mental Health Crisis Among Doctors is a Problem for Patients. Vox. October 25, 2023. www.vox.com/health/23921266/mental-health-doctors-physicians-depression-burnout.

77. Fibuch E, Robertson JJ. Dealing Fairly with Disruptive Physicians. *Physician Leadership Journal.* 2019; 6(2):58–61.

78. Hougaard R, Carter J. Ego Is the Enemy of Good Leadership. *Harvard Business Review.* November 6, 2018. https://hbr.org/2018/11/ego-is-the-enemy-of-good-leadership.

79. Owen D. *The Hubris Syndrome: Bush, Blair and the intoxication of Power.* Methuen: North Yorkshire, UK;2012.

80. Owen D, Davidson J. Hubris Syndrome: An Acquired Personality Disorder? *Brain.* 2009;132(5): 1396–1406. https://doi.org/10.1093/brain/awp008.

81. Pichert JW, Hickson GB, Moore IN. Using Patient Complaints To Promote Patient Safety: The Patient Advocacy Reporting System (PARS). From *Advances in Patient Safety: New Directions and Alternative Approaches.* Bethesda MD: Agency for Healthcare Research and Quality;2008.

82. Holmes J, Olson L. Dealing with Disruptive Physicians. Medical Group Management Association. May 1, 2016. https://www.mgma.com/articles/dealing-with-disruptive-physicians.

83. Roback H, Strassberg D, Ianelli RJ, Finlayson AJR, Blanco M, Neufield M. Problematic Physicians: A Comparison of Personality Profiles by Offence Type. *Can J Psychiatry.* 2007;52(5):315–322. https://doi.org/10.1177/070674370705200506.

84. Hicks R, McCracken J. Personality Traits of a Disruptive Physician. *Physician Executive.* 2012;38(5):66–69.

85. Mazurek M. *Physicians and Professional Behavior Management Strategies: A Leadership Roadmap and Guide with Case Studies.* Tampa FL: American Association for Physician Leadership;2022.

86. Reynolds NT. Disruptive Physician Behavior: Use and Misuse of the Label. *Journal of Medical Regulation.* 2012;98(1):8–19. https://doi.org/10.30770/2572-1852-98.1.8.

87. Stoner CR, Stoner JS. *Building Leaders: Paving the Path for Emerging Leaders.* New York: Routledge;2013. https://doi.org/10.4324/9780203182574

88. Kets de Vries M, Engellau E. A Clinical Approach to the Dynamics of Leadership and Executive Transformation. In: Nohria N, Khurana R (eds.). *Handbook of Leadership Theory and Practice.* Boston: Harvard Business Press;2010:183–222.

89. Goleman D. *Social Intelligence: The New Science of Social Relationships.* New York: Bantam Dell;2006.

90. Van Rooy D, Viswesveran C. Emotional Intelligence: A Meta-analytic Investigation of Predictive Validity and Nomological Net. *Journal of Vocational Behavior.* 2004;65(1):71–95. https://doi.org/10.1016/S0001-8791(03)00076-9.

91. Kouzes JM, Posner BZ. *The Leadership Challenge: How to Get Extraordinary Things Done in Organizations.* San Francisco: Jossey-Bass;1995.

92. Patterson K, Grenny J, McMillan R, Switzler A. *Crucial Conversations: Tools for Talking When The Stakes Are High.* New York: McGraw-Hill;2012.

93. Stone D, Patton B, Heen S. *Difficult Conversations: How to Discuss What Matters Most.* New York: Penguin;2010.

94. Reynolds M. *The Discomfort Zone: How Leaders Turn Difficult Conversations into Breakthroughs.* San Francisco: Berrett-Koehler;2014.

95. Flagg D. *Surviving Dreaded Conversations: Talk Through Any Difficult Situation at Work.* New York: McGraw-Hill;2009.

96. Patterson K, Grenny J, Maxfield D, McMillan R, Switzler A. *Crucial Accountability: Tools for Resolving Violated Expectations, Broken Commitments, and Bad Behavior (2nd ed.).* New York: McGraw Hill;2013.

97. Mennino SF, Rubin BA, Brayfield A. Home -to-Job and Job-to-Home Spillover: The Impact of Company Policies and Workplace Culture. *The Sociological Quarterly.* 2005;46(1):107–135. https://doi.org/10.1111/j.1533-8525.2005.00006.x.

98. Goleman D, Boyatzis R, McKee A. *Primal Leadership: Realizing the Power of Emotional Intelligence.* Cambridge, MA: Harvard Business School Press;2002.

99. Hamlin RG, Ellinger AD, Beattie RS. Coaching at the Heart of Managerial Effectiveness: A Cross-Cultural Study of Managerial Behaviors. *Human Resource Development International.* 2006;9(3):305–331. https://doi.org/10.1080/13678860600893524.

100. Gentry WA, Manning B, Wolfe A, Hernez-Broome G, Allen L. What Coaches Believe Are Best Practices for Coaching: A Qualitative Study of Interviews from Coaches in Asia And Europe. *Journal of Leadership Studies.* 2013;7:18–31. https://doi.org/10.1002/jls.21285.

101. Beattie RS, Kim S, Hagen MS, Ellinge AD, Hamlin, RG. Managerial Coaching: A Review of the Empirical Literature and Development of a Model to Guide Future

Practice. *Advances in Developing Human Resources.* 2014;16(2):184–201. https://doi.org/10.1177/1523422313520476.

102. Center for Creative Leadership. Coaching to Improve Performance & Provide Support. Center for Creative Leadership. April 9, 2020. www.ccl.org/articles/leading-effectively-articles/coaching-to-improve-performance/.

103. Keil A. *Coaching for Leaders: Why Executives Need Support.* Center for Creative Leadership. June 24, 2021. www.ccl.org/articles/white-papers/coaching-for-leaders/.

104. Dyrbye LS. Effect of Professional Coaching Intervention on the Well-Being and Distress of Physicians: A Pilot Randomized Clinical Trial. *JAMA Internal Medicine.* 2019;179(10):1406–1414. https://doi.org/10.1001/jamainternmed.2019.2425.

105. Nemecek P. The Decision Bridge: A Model for Coaching Distressed Physicians. *International Journal of Evidence Based Coaching and Mentoring.* 2023;S17:108–121.

106. Nohria N, Khurana R (eds.). *Handbook of Leadership Theory and Practice.* Boston: Harvard Business Press;2010.

107. Bozer G, Jones RJ. Understanding the Factors That Determine Workplace Coaching Effectiveness: A Systematic Literature Review. *European Journal of Work and Organizational Psychology.* 2018;27(3):342–361. https://doi.org/10.1080/135943 2X.2018.1446946.

108. Rousseau DM, Sitkin SB, Burt RS, Camerer C. Not So Different After All: A Cross-Discipline View of Trust. *Academy of Management Review.* 1998;23(3):393–404. https://doi.org/10.5465/amr.1998.926617.

109. Assay P, Lambert MJ. The Empirical Case for the Common Factors in Therapy: Qualitative Findings. In: Hubble MA, Duncan BL, Miller SD (eds). *The Heart and Soul of Change: What Works in Therapy.* Washington, DC: American Psychological Association;1999:23–55. https://doi.org/10.1037/11132-001.

110. Eisenberger R, Stinglhamber F, Vandenberghe C, Sucharski IL, Rhoades L. Perceived Supervisor Support: Contributions to Perceived Organizational Support and Employee Retention. *Journal of Applied Psychology.* 2002;87(3):565–573. https://doi.org/10.1037/0021-9010.87.3.565.

111. Kurtesses JN, Eisenberger R, Ford MT, Buffardi LC, Stewart KA, Adis CS. Perceived Organizational Support: A Meta-analytic Evaluation of Organizational Support Theory. *Journal of Management.* 2017;43(6): 1854–1884. https://doi.org/10.1177/0149206315575554.

112. Patterson K, Grenny J, Maxfield D, McMillan R, Switzler A. *Influencer: The Power to Change Anything (2nd ed.).* New York: McGraw Hill;2013.

113. David S. *Emotional Agility: Get Unstuck, Embrace Change, and Thrive in Work and Life.* New York: Penguin;2016.

114. Stone D, Patton B, Heen S. *Difficult Conversations: How to Discuss What Matters Most.* New York: Penguin;2010.

115. Boyatzis R, Smith ML, Van Oosten E. *Helping People Change: Coaching with Compassion for Lifelong Learning and Growth.* Boston: Harvard Business Review Press;2019.

116. International Coaching Federation. ICF Core Competencies. https://coachingfederation.org/credentials-and-standards/core-competencies.

117. Whitmore J, Kauffman C, David SA. GROW Grows Up: From Winning the Game to Pursuing Transpersonal Goals. In: Whitmore J, Kauffman C, David SA (eds.). *Beyond Goals*. New York: Routledge;2016:245–260.

118. Batista E. 2015. Giving Feedback That Sticks. *HBR Guide to Coaching Employees*. Boston: Harvard Business Review Press;2015.

119. Trezeciak S, Mazzarelli A. *Compassionomics: The Revolutionary Scientific Evidence That Caring Makes a Difference*. Chicago: Huron Consulting Services;2019.

120. Goleman D. *Focus: The Hidden Driver of Excellence*. New York: Harper;2015.

121. Locke EA, Latham GP. Building a Practically Useful Theory of Goal Setting and Task Performance. *American Psychologist*. 2002;57(9)705–717. https://doi.org/10.1037//0003-066X.57.9.705.

122. Ibarra H, Scoular A. The Leader as Coach. *Harvard Business Review*. 2019;97(6):110–119.

123. Whitmore J. *Coaching for Performance: Growing Human Potential and Purpose—The Principles and Practice of Coaching and Leadership*. London: Nicholas Brealey Publishing;2010.

124. Schein EH. *Humble Inquiry: The Gentle Art of Asking Instead of Telling*. San Francisco: Berrett-Koehler;2013.

125. Duhigg C. *Supercommunicators: How to Unlock the Secret Language of Connection*. New York: Random House;2024.

126. Kotter JP. Leading Change: Why Transformational Efforts Fail. *Harvard Business Review on Change*. Boston: Harvard Business School Publishing;1998.

127. Ertz M, Early PC, Hulin CI. The Impact of Participation on Goal Acceptance and Performance: A Two-Step Model. *Academy of Management Journal*. 1985;28(1):50–66. https://doi.org/10.2307/256061.

128. Ordóñez LD, Schweitzer ME, Galinsky AD, Bazerman MH. Goals Gone Wild: The Systematic Side Effects of Overprescribing Goal Setting. *Academy of Management Perspectives*. 2009;23(1):6–16. https://doi.org/10.5465/amp.2009.37007999.

129. Sheff RA, Sagin T. *A Practical Guide to Preventing and Solving Disruptive Physician Behavior*. Middleton MA: HC Pro Inc.;2004.

130. Sinek S. *Start with Why: How Great Leaders Inspire Everyone to Take Action*. London: Portfolio;2009.

131. Neuhaus M. Cognitive Dissonance: Theory, Examples & How to Reduce It. Positive Psychology. February 8, 2021. https://positivepsychology.com/cognitive-dissonance-theory.

132. Doran G. There's a S.M.A.R.T. Way to Write Management's Goals and Objectives. *Management Review*. 1981;70(11):35–36.

133. Rosenstein AH, Karwaki T, King K. Legal Entanglements in Dealing with Disruptive Behavior. *Physician Leadership Journal*. 2016;3(3), 46-51.

134. Santin BJ, Kaups KL. The Disruptive Physician: Addressing the Issues. *Bulletin of the FACS*. 2015; 100(2):20–24.

135. Veenstra GL, Dabekaussen KFAA, Molleman E, Heineman E, Welker GA. Health Care Professionals' Motivation, Their Behaviors, and the Quality of Hospital Care: A

Mixed-Methods Systematic Review. *Health Care Management Review.* 2022;47(2)155–167. https://doi.org/10.1097/HMR.0000000000000284.

136. Gottman JM, DeClaire J, Gottman J. *The Relationship Cure.* New York: Three Rivers Press;2001.

137. Cuddy AJC, Kohut M, Neffinger J. Connect, the Lead. *Harvard Business Review.* 2013;91(7/8):54–61.

138. Amabile T, Kramer S. *The Progress Principle: Using Small Wins to Ignite Joy, Encouragement, and Creativity at Work.* Boston: Harvard Business Review Press;2011.

139. Goleman D. *Emotional Intelligence: Why It Can Matter More Than IQ.* New York: Bantam Books;2005.

140. Mayer JD, Goleman D, Barrett C, Gutstein S. Leading by Feel. *Harvard Business Review.* 2004;82(1):27–27.

141. Eurich T. What Self-Awareness Really Is (and How to Cultivate It). *Harvard Business Review.* January 4, 2018:4.

142. Bar-On R. *The Emotional Quotient Inventory.* North Towanda, NY: Multi-Help Systems;2002:18. https://doi.org/10.1037/t03760-000

143. Joseph DL, Newman DA. Emotional Intelligence: An Integrative Meta-Analysis and Cascading Model. *Journal of Applied Psychology.* 2010;95(1):54–78. https://doi.org/10.1037/a0017286.

144. Trivers R. *The Folly of Fools: The Logic of Self-Deception in Human Life.* New York: Basic Books/Hachette Book Group;2011.

145. Festinger L. *A Theory of Cognitive Dissonance.* Stanford, CA: Stanford University Press:1957.

146. Baron-Cohen S. The Empathy Bell Curve. *Phi Kappa Phi Forum.* 2011;91(12):50–60:55. https://doi.org/10.1515/9781503620766.

147. Staw BM. Knee-Deep in the Big Muddy: A Study of the Escalating Commitment to a Chosen Course of Action. *Organizational Behavior and Human Performance.* 1976;16(1):27–44. https://doi.org/10.1016/0030-5073(76)90005-2.

148. Goleman D. The Focused Leader. *Harvard Business Review.* 2013;91(12):50–60.

149. Goleman D. What Is Empathy? *Empathy: HBR Emotional Intelligence Series.* Boston: Harvard Business Review Press;2017.

150. Fisher R, Ury W, Patton B. *Getting to Yes: Negotiating Agreement without Giving In.* New York: Viking Penguin;1991.

151. Covey SR. *The 7 Habits of Highly Successful People: Powerful Lessons in Personal Change.* New York: Fireside;1989:239.

152. Stoner CR, Gilligan JF. *The Adversity Challenge: How Successful Leaders Bounce Back from Setbacks.* Provo UT: Executive Excellence Publications;2006.

153. Frei F, Morriss A. Begin with Trust. *Harvard Business Review.* 2020;98(3):112–121.

154. Zenger J, Folkman J. The 3 Elements of Trust. *Harvard Business Review.* February 5, 2019. http://hbr.org/2019/02/the-3-elements-of-trust.

155. Bandelli AC. *Relational Intelligence: The Five Essential Skills You Need to Build Life-Changing Relationships.* Murrell's Inlet, SC: Covenant Books;2022.

156. Meglino BM, Korsgaard A. Considering Rationale Self-Interest as a Disposition: Organizational Implications of Other Orientation. Journal of Applied Psychology. 2004;89(6):946–959. https://psycnet.apa.org/doi/10.1037/0021-9010.89.6.946.

157. Tuckman B. Developmental Sequence in Small Groups. *Psychological Bulletin*. 1965;63(6): 384–399. https://doi.org/10.1037/h0022100.

158. Lencioni P.M. The Five Dysfunctions of a Team: A Leadership Fable. New York: John Wiley & Sons;2010.

159. Katzenbach JR, Smith DK. *The Wisdom of Teams: Creating the High-Performance Organization*. Boston, MA: Harvard Business Review Press;2015.

160. Lewicki RJ, Brinsfield C. Trust Repair. *Annual Review of Organizational Psychology and Organizational Behavior*. 2017;4:287–313. https://doi.org/10.1146/annurev-orgpsych-032516-113147.

161. Gallo A. What Is Psychological Safety? *Harvard Business Review*. February 15, 2023. https://hbr.org/2023/02/what-is-psychological-safety.

162. McKinsey & Company. Psychological Safety and the Critical Role of Leadership Development. February 11, 2001. https://www.mckinsey.com/capabilities/people-and-organizational-performance/our-insights/psychological-safety-and-the-critical-role-of-leadership-development#/

163. Peterson R, Shah PP, Ferguson AJ, Jones S. 4 Common Types of Team Conflict — and How to Resolve Them. *Harvard Business Review*. May 7, 2024. https://hbr.org/2024/05/4-common-types-of-team-conflict-and-how-to-resolve-them

164. Thompson L. What To Do When You Have a Dysfunctional Team Member. *Harvard Business Review*. May 16, 2017. https://hbr.org/sponsored/2017/05/what-to-do-when-you-have-a-dysfunctional-team-member.

165. Sherif CW, Sherif M, Nebergall RE. *Attitude and Attitude Change: The Social Judgment Involvement Approach*. Philadelphia: Saunders;1965.

166. Bohnet I. How to Take the Bias Out of Interviews. *Harvard Business Review*. April 18, 2016. https://hbr.org/2016/04/how-to-take-the-bias-out-of-interviews.

167. Dust S. What Is Job Fit and Why Does It Matter. *Psychology Today*. October 20, 2020. https://www.psychologytoday.com/us/blog/what-we-really-want-in-a-leader/202010/what-is-job-fit-and-why-does-it-matter.

168. Brown AK, Schneider B. Person-Organization Fit Theory and Research: Conundrums, Conclusions and Calls To Action. *Personnel Psychology*. February 11, 2023. https://doi.org/10.1111/peps.12581.

169. Cable DM, Parsons CK. 2001. Socialization Tactics and Person-Organization Fit. *Personnel Psychology*. 2001;54(1):1–23. https://doi.org/10.1111/j.1744-6570.2001.tb00083.x.

170. Millette TE, Kruse K. *How to Fire an Employee: The Right Way to Terminate Someone*. Philadelphia: LEADx;2017.

171. Merrick C. 6 Ways to Reinvigorate Your Team After Firing an Employee. *Entrepreneur*. October 28, 2016. Accessed August 30, 2024. https://www.entrepreneur.com/leadership/6-ways-to-reinvigorate-your-team-after-firing-an-employee/28402.

172. Reserva J. How to Terminate an Employee: Essential Dos and Don'ts. *Workforce.* August 12, 2024. https://workforce.com/news/how-to-terminate-an-employee.

173. Drainville B. How to Talk to Your Team About a Terminated Employee. Timesheet Mobile Blog. October 11, 2017. Accessed August 30, 2024. https://blog.timesheetmobile.com/how-to-talk-to-your-team-about-a-terminated-employee.

174. Graen GB, Uhl-Bien M. The Relationship-Based Approach to Leadership: Development of LMX Theory Over 25 Years. *The Leadership Quarterly.* 1995;67(2):219–247. https://doi.org/10.1016/1048-9843(95)90036-5.

175. Anisman-Razin M, Kark R, Ashforth BE. Doing Distance: The Role of Managements' Enactment of Psychological Distance in Leader-Follower Relationships. *Group & Organization Management.* June 2, 2023. https://doi.org/10.1177/10596011231158264.

176. Antonakis J, Atwater L. Leader Distance: A Review and a Proposed Theory. *The Leadership Quarterly.* 2002;13(6):673–704. https://doi.org/10.1016/S1048-9843(02)00155-8.

177. Huseman R, Hatfield J, Miles E. A New Perspective on Equity Theory: The Equity Sensitivity Construct. *Academy of Management Review.* 1987;12:232–234. https://doi.org/10.2307/258531.

178. Hill LA, Lineback K. *Being the Boss: The 3 Imperatives for Being a Great Leader.* Boston: Harvard Business Review Press;2011:52.

179. Gabarro JJ, Kotter JP. Managing Your Boss. *Harvard Business Review.* 2005;83(1):92–99.

180. Burns E. How to Sell Your Ideas Up the Chain of Command. *Harvard Business Review.* 2022;100(1):139–143.

181. Kahneman D. *Thinking, Fast and Slow.* New York: Farrar, Straus, and Giroux;2011.

182. Grant A. *Think Again: The Power of Knowing What You Don't Know.* New York: Viking;2022.

183. Weick KE. The Collapse of Sensemaking in Organizations: The Mann Gulch Disaster. *Administrative Science Quarterly.* 1993;38:628–652. https://doi.org/10.2307/2393339.

www.ingramcontent.com/pod-product-compliance
Lightning Source LLC
Chambersburg PA
CBHW070731220326
41598CB00024BA/3393